CARMEL IN

"I CONSIDER T ⋯⋯ ⊥

a mini-cours ⋯⋯ ⊥ᴜⱼ Castle

Joel Giallanza, C.S.C.

"I CONSIDER THE LABOR WELL SPENT"

a mini-course on the Interior Castle

Edizioni Carmelitane

Roma

4

Copyright © by Edizioni Carmelitane. All rights reserved. No part of this publication may be reproduced, stored in a retrieval system, or transmitted, in any form or by any means, electronic, mechanical, photocopying, recording, or otherwise, without the prior written permission of the publisher.

First Printing: 2001
Second Printing: 2005

ISBN 88-7288-066-1
ISSN 0394-7750

© Edizioni Carmelitane
Via Sforza Pallavicini, 10
00193 Roma

Finito di stampare nel luglio 2005
dalla Tipografia Città Nuova della P.A.M.O.M.
Via S. Romano in Garfagnana, 23
00148 Roma - tel. 066530467
e-mail: segr.tipografia@cittanuova.it

INTRODUCTION

"I consider the labor well spent."[1] This is Saint Teresa of Avila's own assessment of writing the *Interior Castle*. This is a particularly positive evaluation considering that she began the writing project by saying, "I don't think I have much more to say" (*Prologue*, 2). Fortunately, she did have more to say and, in the process, composed one of the most important classics within the mystical tradition of the church.

The following chapters are presented as a mini-course on this classic of Christian spirituality. This overview article will serve as a general introduction to Saint Teresa of Avila and to the *Interior Castle*. Each of the next seven chapters will examine one of the mansions described by Teresa. A final chapter will conclude the study. My hope in this series is to provide readers with the basic background necessary for reading the *Interior Castle* with an awareness of the fundamental principles which Saint Teresa incorporates into her work and which are important for understanding Teresian spirituality.

TERESA DE AHUMADA

Writings on the life of Saint Teresa and on the sixteenth-century Spanish world in which she lived are ample and accessible; biographies as well as her own writings are available in almost every language. To offer an extensive study into Teresa's life

---

[1]. *Interior Castle*, Epilogue, 1. All texts are taken from *The Collected Works of St. Teresa of Avila*, translated by Kieran Kavanaugh, O.C.D. and Otilio Rodriguez, O.C.D.; Washington, D.C.: Institute of Carmelite Studies; ICS Publications, 1976. All texts from the *Interior Castle* will be annotated with a Roman numeral to indicate the specific mansion, and two numbers separated by a colon to indicate the chapter and paragraph.

and world is beyond the scope of this present work. What follows is simply a brief outline of her life as seen through five major periods.

1515-1536 - Teresa is born on Sunday, 28 March 1515 of Alonso and Beatriz de Ahumada. Her father had two children by a previous marriage; when his wife died, he remarried and had ten more children of whom Teresa is the third. There was no system of public education in Spain at the time; nevertheless, Teresa received a rudimentary education at home until she was sixteen. Then, Alonso entrusted his daughter's further education to the Augustinian nuns of Our Lady of Grace in Avila. In time, Teresa began to consider the possibility of a religious vocation. Her father refused. On 2 November 1535, she "ran away from home" so to speak, to enter the Carmelite monastery of the Incarnation in Avila. Her father acceded to her wishes and even provided a generous dowry for her entrance. Thus begins her life in the tradition of Carmel as Sister Teresa of Jesus.

1536-1538 - After her profession of vows in 1537, Teresa's early religious life is marked by an intense fervor for perfection and prayer. This period is also marked by an illness which, in varying degrees, remains with Teresa for the rest of her life. The initial sign was a type of complete exhaustion, brought on by her intense desire to please God combined with the austere food and lifestyle at the Incarnation monastery. The medical treatments over a period of three months did nothing to improve her health. In fact, they added to its diminishment, leaving her unable to walk for three years. Teresa herself testified that it was through the intercession of Saint Joseph that she was able to walk again.

1538-1556 - This period of eighteen years is marked by spiritual dryness. Prayer became increasingly difficult and even dissatisfying. In her

Life she writes, "so unbearable was the sadness I felt on entering the oratory, that I had to muster up all my courage" (8:7). Her fidelity to prayer was often sustained through reading a book. But faithful she remained. Once while praying before an image of the wounded Christ she experienced a profound realization of the need to place all her trust in God and not in her own abilities and efforts. This realization heralds a new period of her life.

1556-1562 - These years are characterized by intense growth in Teresa's mystical life, including such experiences as visions and locutions. This was a time of conversion for Teresa, an entrance into the supernatural dimensions of the spiritual life. She described these dimensions as supernatural because she knew that she could not acquire or generate such experiences through her "natural" efforts. Desiring to live in the Carmelite tradition as intensely as possible, Teresa asks her superiors for permission to found a convent under the "Primitive Rule." This project is realized on 24 August 1562 when four novices receive the habit in the new monastery of Saint Joseph, in Avila. It is not until December that Teresa herself receives permission to move to the monastery.

1562-1582 - During the final twenty years of her life, Teresa is involved in obtaining formal approval for the new monastery as well as in founding a variety of other monasteries in Spain. Of necessity, then, Teresa travels a great deal during this period, forming and reforming convents. Her health begins to show increasing signs of instability as she weakened with fevers and various other physical difficulties. During this period (1567) she meets Saint John of the Cross and convinces him to join her in the work of Reform she has undertaken. Her health becomes increasingly unstable and leads to her death at nine o'clock in the evening on Monday, 4 October 1582 at sixty-seven years of age.

To complete this very brief outline it can be added that Teresa was beatified on 24 April 1614 by Pope Paul V; canonized on 12 March 1622 by Pope Gregory XV; and declared (the first woman) Doctor of the Church on 27 September 1970 by Pope Paul VI.

WRITINGS

Given all the activities in which Saint Teresa was involved during her sixty-seven years, it is hard to imagine that she found time to write of her experiences. And yet, write she did: letters, poetry, constitutions for her religious community, meditations, and several major works of considerable significance in the mystical tradition of the church. What follows is a simple overview of those major writings.

Saint Teresa began to write her *Life* in 1562. This work deals with spiritual and mystical graces received by Teresa. In this writing she incorporates autobiographical material spanning the years from her early childhood until 1565. In 1566 she writes the *Way of Perfection* which describes the way of life leading to union with God. Teresa's reflections on and recounting of the experiences related to her *Foundations* were written in 1573. The *Interior Castle* was written in 1577. It is not possible to give a precise date for Teresa's *Spiritual Testimonies* which could be considered a sequel to the *Life*, covering the years 1560-1579. The lack of precision in dating this work is due to the fact that it is a collection of reflections written at different periods during those nineteen years.

It must be noted that the dates provided here indicate when Teresa began to write each of these works. Her writing projects were undertaken in response to the directives she received from her "confessors" (spiritual directors) over the years; they believed it important that she write of her experiences. In the midst of her travels and the other responsibilities associated with the Reform, Teresa would further edit her writings after they had been reviewed by her current confessor and often by several other people. After all, Saint Teresa is living during the time of the Spanish Inquisition and it was important to say all things "in conformity with what the holy Roman Catholic Church holds" (*Interior Castle*, Prologue, 3). Several of her own works were scrutinized by the Inquisitors.

Saint Teresa's style of writing in spontaneous and free-spirited, reflecting the way she spoke. It displays her personality as an extravert individual whose usual disposition was cheerful and friendly and ever ready to engage in conversation. This characteristic style of writing is important to keep in mind when reading Saint Teresa's works. Unlike more systematic writers, Teresa is content to begin a series of points and not complete it. Her travels frequently interrupted her writing for months at a time. When she could take pen in hand again, usually, she did not review where she had left off. In fact, sometimes she could not, since the completed portion of a manuscript may have already been dispatched to her confessor for review.

INTERIOR CASTLE

In May, 1577, Saint Teresa was speaking to her confessor, Father Jerome Gratian, about her spiritual experiences. He asked her to elaborate on one point so he could explain it to the sisters who had been asking him about the spiritual life. Teresa commented that she had already explained the point in question very well in the *Life*. But Father Gratian could not look up this information since the manuscript was being examined by the Inquisition. So, he orders her to write another work; that order results in what came to be known as the book of the *Dwelling Places*, or the *Interior Castle*.

Saint Teresa of Avila began writing the *Interior Castle* on 2 June 1577. She completed her writing on 29 November 1577. Given the extent of this writing and the complexity of the experiences Teresa is describing, those seven months seem an incredibly short span of time. And yet, even to say seven months is inaccurate. With the interruptions she experienced during this period, either because of pressing matters related to the Reform or because of her declining health, the actual writing time for the *Interior Castle* was approximately two months!

How did such a spiritual masterpiece come into existence so quickly? Teresa explained to one of her first biographers, Father Diego de Yepes, that God showed her the entire book in a flash. Father Diego recounts:

> There was a most beautiful crystal globe like a castle in which she saw seven dwelling places, and in the seventh, which was in the center, the King of Glory dwelt in the greatest splendor. From there He beautified and illumined all those dwelling places to the outer wall. The inhabitants received more light the nearer they were to the center. Outside of the castle was all darkness, with toads, vipers, and other poisonous vermin.

In the very first chapter of the *Interior Castle*, Teresa reiterates this by saying "Our soul is like a castle made entirely out of a diamond or of very clear crystal, in which there are many rooms, just as in heaven there are many dwelling places" (I,1:1). And again, "Well, let us consider that this castle has, as I said, many dwelling places: some up above, others down below, others to the sides; and in the center and middle is the main dwelling place where the very secret exchanges between God and the soul take place" (I,1:3). Those "many dwelling places" refer to different stages and spiritual experiences within an individual's journey toward union with God who ever dwells at the center of the castle. Thus, the *Interior Castle* deals with the practice and experience of prayer and the spiritual life from beginning to perfection.

It is not surprising, then, that Saint Teresa believed this was her finest writing, expressing well her understanding of and experience in the spiritual life. In one letter she compares it to the *Life* by saying, "Personally, I think the book I wrote later (*Interior Castle*) is the better...I have had more experience since I wrote the first" (14 January 1580). In writing to a person who has a copy of the manuscript, Teresa notes that she "has reached the point described in that (7th) Mansion and is experiencing the peace which goes with it; so that she lives a very restful life and eminently learned men say she is making good progress" (8 November 1581). This second quote is particularly important because it verifies that Teresa is writing from her own spiritual experiences. The *Interior Castle* is not a book of theoretical possibilities, but of practical insight into the graced workings of God within the spiritual life.

EXPLORING THE MANSIONS

The term "mansions" was applied to the English versions of Teresa's seven stages using the traditional translation of John 14:2: "In my Father's house there are many mansions."[2] However, the Spanish terms originally used by Teresa refer to "dwelling places" within the castle and not to the stately resi-

---

[2] Saint Teresa alludes to this gospel text in I,1:1.

dences usually denoted by the word mansions. Contemporary English translations of John's gospel often refer to the "many dwelling places in God's house." In these present articles, "mansions" and "dwelling places" will be used interchangeably to blend the terminology already familiar to readers of Teresa with the basic image underlying the stages within the *Interior Castle*.

As noted earlier, the following chapters will examine each of the seven mansions described by Saint Teresa. Specifically, three points will be developed for each mansion. First, a general overview of the mansion will be presented, providing a basic profile of the characteristics identifying that particular mansion. Second, a basic profile of the types and experiences of prayer within that mansion. Third, a basic profile of ways in which the person relates to others, at that particular point in the spiritual life. Because the specific content of the second and third points varies from individual to individual, it will be presented in the first person singular so the reader can make any personally helpful adaptations and applications.

It is very important to note that these points are basic profiles, presenting only an overview of the mansions and the characteristic experiences which individuals encounter within each mansion. This is significant for two reasons. First, these present chapters cannot replace reading and reflecting upon the *Interior Castle* itself. Readers of Teresa's own words will be touched in ways which can give them deeper insights into God's presence and activity in their lives. Second, the comments on prayer and relationships presented in this study cannot be used as a gauge to judge oneself or others in terms of spiritual progress, nor as a criterion to determine exactly which mansion oneself or another is currently experiencing. As was noted above, the *Interi-*

or Castle is not a book of theoretical possibilities; however, neither is it a book of recipes. The following chapters are designed simply to be an introduction to Saint Teresa's great work, to stimulate reflection on the spiritual life as presented in that work, and to encourage further exploration of the teachings from this Doctor of the Church.

As she is concluding her Prologue to the *Interior Castle*, Saint Teresa insists "it's nonsense to think that what I say could matter to other persons. Our Lord will be granting me favor enough if some of these nuns benefit by praising Him a little more. His Majesty well knows that I don't aim after anything else" (4). Clearly, here is one instance where history has proven Teresa wrong. What she says in the *Interior Castle* has indeed mattered to and made a difference in the lives of countless individuals for more than four centuries. And, no doubt, her words will continue to be a guide for those who sincerely choose to make the journey toward union with God, those who strive to spend their lives "praising Him a little more." They, too, will consider the journey into the *Interior Castle* a "labor well spent."

"HOW NECESSARY THIS ROOM IS"

FIRST MANSION

"How necessary this room is." At first glance, this seems like a statement of the obvious; after all, this is the *first* mansion and we have to begin here. Saint Teresa, however, is speaking from another perspective. This is the mansion of self-knowledge. Teresa is very explicit in terms of the necessity of this discipline.

> How necessary this room is - see that you under-stand me - even for those whom the Lord has brought into the very dwelling place where He abides. For never, however exalted the soul may be, is anything else fitting for it; nor could it be even were the soul to so desire (I,2:8).

Though other aspects of and activities within the spiritual life will occupy us for a time as we journey through the *Interior Castle*, self-knowledge remains a permanent part of that journey and is among the principal foundations of Teresian spirituality.

SELF-KNOWLEDGE

Why is self-knowledge so important? God dwells in the central rooms of the castle, deep within us, at the center of the self. We come to the knowledge of God through our efforts to know ourselves. For Saint Teresa, this is simple and direct logic: "Let's strive to make more progress in self-knowledge. In my opinion we shall never completely know ourselves if we don't strive to know God" (I,2:9). As we seek knowledge of God, we grow in self-knowledge; and as we grow in self-knowledge, we deepen our knowledge of God.

Further, in the process of knowing ourselves and knowing God who is within us, we progress in our awareness of the similarity and distinction between God and ourselves. We are similar to God for that is the image and likeness in which we were created. Because we are creatures, this similarity is, simultaneously, the distinction.

> Since this castle is a creature and the difference, therefore, between it and God is the same as that between the Creator and His creature, His Majesty in saying that the soul is made in His own image makes it almost impossible for us to understand the sublime dignity and beauty of the soul (I,1:1).

It follows, then, that a full comprehension of our own soul is equivalent to a full comprehension of God. Clearly, both lie far beyond any point at which we would think we have achieved such comprehension. Self-knowledge and God-knowledge are never-ending.

This is precisely why Saint Teresa insists on the constant importance and necessity of self-knowledge; there is never a point at which it can be casually set aside if we wish to progress. The clearer we see and know who God is and who we are, the deeper will be our humility, our awareness of dependence on God for all things. Thus, self-knowledge is intrinsically bound to humility.

> Knowing ourselves is something so important that I wouldn't want any relaxation ever in this regard, however high you may have climbed into the heavens. While we are on this earth nothing is more important to us than humility. So I repeat that it is good, indeed very good, to try to enter first into the room where self-knowledge is dealt with rather than fly off to other rooms. This is the right road (I,2:9)

Teresian spirituality is incarnational. God dwells at the center of the self; thus, it is by going through and knowing the self that we come to union with and knowledge of God. This incarnational perspective has profound implications. The beauty and majesty of God radiate outward from the central dwelling place, communicating those same qualities to the soul. Our dignity and capacity as human beings are reflections of God's presence and activity within us, of God's beauty and majesty. As Saint Teresa writes, "I don't find anything comparable to the magnificent beauty of a soul and its marvelous capacity" (I,1:1).

The dignity of our nature is irrevocable for it reflects the eternal beauty of God in whose image we are created. "It should be kept in mind here that the fount, the shining sun that is in the center of the soul, does not lose its beauty and splendor; it is always present in the soul, and nothing can take away its loveliness" (I,2:3). As for its capacity, "The soul is capable of much more than we can imagine, and the sun that is in this royal chamber shines in all parts. It is very important for any soul that practices prayer, whether little or much, not to hold itself back and stay in one corner" (I,2:8).

We are created in the image of God, with the capacity for God. This image, this dignity and capacity are stimulants for continued growth. Our awareness of them will clarify and deepen as we take up and remain faithful to the discipline of knowing ourselves. Therefore, we do not need to hold back and stay in one corner, "self-knowledge will not make one base and cowardly" (I,2:11). As we advance in self-knowledge, we become increasingly bold in doing what needs to be done for continued progress in the spiritual journey.

PRAYER

"Insofar as I can understand the door of entry to this castle is prayer and reflection" (I,1:7). As prayer is the entrance to the castle, so it is for this first mansion. Those who do not pray are "souls so ill and so accustomed to being involved in external matters that there is no remedy, nor does it seem they can enter within themselves" (I,1:6). In fact, "if the Lord doesn't come to order them to get up...they are quite unfortunate and in serious danger;" thus, Teresa continues, "we are speaking to other souls that, in the end, enter the castle" (I,1:8).

There is an important assumption here which must be noted since it holds firm for the first and the remaining mansions as well. In the *Interior Castle*, Teresa is writing for those who pray, she assumes her readers pray and are serious in their efforts to enter the castle and make the spiritual journey as fully as possible. Those who do not pray, do not even enter the castle. Saint Teresa does not write for those who choose not to pray because "what I want to explain to you is very difficult to understand without experience" (I,1:9). And that experience is mediated by prayer.

The prayer and the reflection which Teresa identifies as the doorway to this mansion are inseparably linked.

> I don't mean to refer to mental more than vocal prayer, for since vocal prayer is prayer it must be accompanied by reflection. A prayer in which a person is not aware of whom he is speaking to, what he is asking, who it is who is asking and of whom, I do not call prayer however much the lips move (I,1:7).

The reflection which accompanies prayer, regardless of how simple and scattered it may be initially, is the means through which the process of growth in self-knowledge and humility begins. Through prayer and reflection I come to a first awareness of God within me, of the dignity and capacity of my soul, and of my similarity to and distinction from God.

What is the profile of prayer in this first mansion? From the perspective of regularity, prayer is much more sporadic than steady. The first mansion is a time of wonder and self-discovery. I am learning about who I am and making decisions about what I value. There is a fascination with and focus on self which do not afford me much energy and enthusiasm for prayer. The effort and even the desire are present, but the regularity is not. As Saint Teresa notes of first mansion dwellers, "even though they are very involved in the world, they have good desires and sometimes, though only once in a while, they entrust themselves to our Lord and reflect on who they are, although in a rather hurried fashion" (I,1:8).

Prayer takes time and, at this point in the spiritual journey, I would prefer to expend that time on matters which I have decided are of more value to me. What fidelity there is, however, enables me to enter the mansion.

> During the period of a month they will sometimes pray, but their minds are then filled with business matters which ordinarily occupy them. They are so attached to these things that where their treasure lies their heart goes also. Sometimes they do put all these things aside, and the self-knowledge and awareness that they are not proceeding correctly to get to the door is important. Finally, they enter the first, lower room (I,1:8).

As for the type of prayer in this mansion, it is primarily simple, vocal prayers I learned in childhood or read from a devotional book. My prayer also includes spiritual practices such as participation in church services. As Teresa noted, however, reflection and meditation do accompany this prayer on occasion and give me a glimpse into what must be done if I am to progress in the spiritual life. Sometimes my prayer or other spiritual practices will take momentary priority, even to the point of extremes. But this is usually short-lived and, as a first mansion dweller, I soon return to being "absorbed in the world and engulfed in their pleasures and vanities, with their honors and pretenses" (I,2:12).

RELATIONSHIPS

"True perfection consists in love of God and neighbor; the more perfectly we keep these two commandments the more perfect we will be" (I,2:17). The inconsistencies of my relationship with God are reflected in my relationships with others. Just as sustaining any focus on God is a particular challenge in the first mansion, so too is maintaining any deep relationships with other people. The focus on self becomes the lens through which relationships are viewed, developed, and maintained. Thus, I enjoy and even attract the attention of others insofar as that is a support in life. At the same time I expect that support to be given freely without many or without any demands for reciprocity. My relationships are for me. My focus on self does not give me the freedom to attend to the needs or preferences expressed by those with whom I am in relationship. In fact, my focus on self does not enable me to see and be aware of those needs and preferences.

Though I want the support of others, I am not so quick to extend it. I tend, rather, to stand in judgement of others, scrutinizing their way of living Christianity while giving very little quality attention to my own. The operative mode of interaction becomes competition because it maintains the primary focus for all or most of the attention within the relationship on myself. I remain the standard for how things are to be done. The result of this, according to Saint Teresa, is that "the soul could lose its peace and even disturb the peace of others by going about looking at trifling things in people that at times are not even imperfections, but since we know little we see these things in the worst light" (I,2:18).

Sacrifice and self-renunciation are not a part of my relational behaviors, but I do expect my friends to go out of their way to attend to my needs. Because my relationships are not developed on very deep levels, friends and acquaintances are expendable. If I sense that they are not attentive enough to me or that they are making too many demands for attention from me, I can simply diminish any further pursuit of those relationships, allowing them to end. I prefer and seek the company of others who will share my fascination with myself and allow me to remain an unchallenged center of attention.

Even with all this, I am not completely devoid of generosity. In my relationships - personal and professional - I can and do occasionally extend myself for others. However, this extension is not free of ulterior motives. If whatever I do can bring some personal benefit or professional advancement or public notoriety to me, then I am more than willing to invest my time and energy. If I perceive, though, there will be little or no return on my investment, then the prospect of extending myself in the first place is much less attractive. Thus, even those actions which are genuinely beneficial to others retain some dimension of drawing attention and accolade to the self. The desire to be generous and giving and even selfless is present, but the hesitancy to act on that desire is stronger because of the perceived cost to self-interest.

FIDELITY

The first mansion does not receive very much of the brilliant light emanating from the central dwelling place. So many attachments obscure the light that we cannot see the true beauty and dignity of ourselves and of creation around us, except for the most superficial level. We are not aware of the

> precious things that can be found in this soul, or who dwells within it, or its high value. Consequently, little effort is made to preserve its beauty. All our attention is taken up with the plainness of the diamond's setting or the outer wall of the castle; that is, with these bodies of ours (I,1:2).

Good desires are possible and present in the first mansion, but the discipline and self-renunciation necessary to assure the purity of those desires are not taken up with any consistency or they are not present at all.

First mansion dwellers are within the castle, but only in the foyer, so to speak. The more profound experiences and periods of growth within the spiritual life cannot yet be imagined. Thus, the pathways to continued progress are not clearly seen.

> So, I think, must be the condition of the soul. Even though it may not be in a bad state, it is so involved in worldly things and so absorbed with its possessions, honor, or business affairs...that even though as a matter of fact it would want to see and enjoy its beauty these things do not allow it to; nor does it seem that it can slip free from so many impediments (I,2:14).

To continue the journey, we must remain faithful to our prayer and spiritual practices, however rudimentary they may be. In this way, we open ourselves to the workings of God's grace within us. Fidelity will clarify our self-knowledge and deepen our humility, teaching us just "how necessary this room is" now and for the future. What we learn from that teaching will posture us at the doorway to the second mansion.

"THESE ROOMS INVOLVE MUCH MORE EFFORT"

SECOND MANSION

"These rooms involve much more effort." Those who have grown through their experiences of the first mansion have already begun the discipline of practicing prayer. "But they still don't have the determination to remain in this second stage without turning back, for they don't avoid the occasion of sin" (II,1:2). Thus, there is here more work than previously required to sustain what has begun and to move forward. This is why Saint Teresa notes,

> These rooms, in part, involve much more effort than do the first, even though there is not as much danger, for now it seems that souls in them recognize the dangers, and there is great hope they will enter further into the castle (II,1:2).

The recognition that it is possible to fall back combined with the desire to move forward characterize this as the mansion of understanding desire. We now understand that there is more to the spiritual life than we have experienced thus far, and we desire it, even though we do not yet know all that lies ahead. We have a deepening realization that our continuation of the journey will indeed involve "much more effort."

UNDERSTANDING DESIRE

Of all the mansions, this second mansion is dealt with most briefly by Saint Teresa. The experiences within this mansion surely constitute important components within the spiritual journey. However, Teresa sees them as a logical continuation of the first mansion, thus she does not need to elaborate very extensively on them. At the beginning of this chapter, she tells her readers, "I'd like to say only a little, for I have spoken at length on this subject elsewhere" (II,1:1).[1] This brevity is easy to understand when we recall that Saint Teresa is assuming her readers pray. Apart from that assumption, little of what she says will be comprehensible.

What nurtures this understanding desire? What is the door to this second mansion? Saint Teresa already responded to this near the end of her reflections on the first mansion. "If a person is to enter the second dwelling place, it is important that he strive to give up unnecessary things and business affairs. Each one should do this in conformity with his state in life" (I,2:14). Renunciation is the door to this mansion and a necessary prelude to the next mansion. Our desire to progress in the spiritual life must be confirmed by our efforts. Specifically, those efforts must reflect our willingness to root our identity in the Lord alone and no longer in the "unnecessary things and business affairs" which have been our principal concerns thus far. Our efforts must rest firmly upon our deepening self-knowledge that we are created in the image of God, with the capacity for God. This image and capacity are keys to the understanding desire which characterizes this mansion. They are the foundation and meaning of any renunciation we initiate.

There are many means at our disposal for hearing and responding to God's call, and we are more sensitive to these means in the second mansion. Saint Teresa teaches that we can hear the voice of God

---

[1]. In chapters 11 to 13 of the *Life* Saint Teresa writes of experiences very similar to those she mentions in the first and second mansions. Also, throughout the *Way of Perfection* she writes of what is experienced as individuals progress on the spiritual journey.

through words spoken by other good people, or though sermons, or through what is read in good books, or through the many things that are heard and by which God calls, or through illnesses and trials, or also through a truth that He teaches during the brief moments we spend in prayer; however lukewarm these moments may be, God esteems them highly (II,1:3)

Of course, since we are only in the second mansion, we cannot guarantee that our response to the Lord will be immediate. Renunciation takes time since it leads us from the familiar to the unfamiliar. No matter; provided that our efforts are sincere, the Lord will bless our progress. "His Majesty knows well how to wait many days and years, especially when he sees perseverance and good desires. This perseverance is most necessary here. One always gains much through perseverance" (*ibid.*). As fidelity was important for progress in the first mansion, it is even more so in the second mansion.

The principal challenge confronting us within this second mansion is the determination that turning back is not an option. Arriving at that determination can be quite a struggle. In fact, the person "doesn't know whether to continue or to return to the first room" (II,1:4). Why is this? Primarily because, when we look back on our life to this point, it is easy to interpret "the temporal pleasures of the present as though almost eternal" (*ibid.*). By contrast, when we look forward, it is not so clear what lies ahead if we make the renunciation necessary for continued progress. So, we are torn; we do not know whether to continue or to return. Saint Teresa explains how our reason, faith, memory, will, and intellect assist us in determining to continue our journey and not turn back. The struggle to arrive at that determination is real, but grace is present to assist us if we but trust. "Ah, my Lord! Your help is necessary here; without it one can do nothing" (II,1:6).

Spiritual direction is especially helpful for those in this second mansion as well as in the remaining mansions. It can provide the encouragement and perspective needed for being determined and for remaining faithful.

> It's a wonderful thing for a person to talk to those who speak about this interior castle, to draw near not only to those seen to be in these rooms where he is but to those known to have entered the ones closer to the center. Conversation with these latter will be a great help to him, and he can converse so much with them that they will bring him to where they are (*ibid.*).

For Saint Teresa, the ideal spiritual director combines both knowledge and experience: knowledge of what is involved in the spiritual journey and experience of that journey. In this way, the director can offer a solid guidance based on knowledge and a sound wisdom based on experience, both of which are very helpful to second mansion dwellers.

PRAYER

What is the profile of prayer in this second mansion? "This stage pertains to those who have already begun to practice prayer" (II,1:2). In this mansion, the practice of prayer refers primarily to discursive meditation and simple recollection. My prayer now has that more reflective quality of mental prayer rather than the basic verbal nature of vocal prayer which characterized the first mansion.

Generally, my experience of prayer is pleasant, with occasional consolations. I have an awareness of my spiritual growth and the consolations I experience are a source of affirmation and encouragement. However, this is not always the case. There are times of dryness and uncertainty when I question the value of continuing this journey on which I have set out. The temptation is to assume that consolations should be the norm if growth is truly taking place. However, as Teresa says, "souls shouldn't be thinking about consolations at this beginning stage. It would be a very poor way to start building so precious and great an edifice" (II,1:7). Saint Teresa of Avila is a realist, growth in prayer and in the spiritual life encompasses both, periods of consolations and of dryness. Expecting anything else is simply unrealistic and even a form of pride.

> It's an amusing thing that even though we still have a thousand impediments and imperfections and our virtues have hardly begun to grow - and please God they may have begun - we are yet not ashamed to seek spiritual delights in prayer or to complain about dryness. May this never happen to you (*ibid.*).

My fidelity to prayer remains inconsistent. I want to be faithful to prayer, but I really do not know how much I actually want it to affect my life. I am uncertain about my readiness and willingness to change my lifestyle. Still, I am attracted to spiritual reading, discussions with my spiritual director, and to conversations with others who value the spiritual life. I want to become a better person; I want to intensify my commitment to the spiritual life. But my biggest weakness is lack of consistency. However, little by little, I am making the necessary effort and I do see some progress. I need to remain more focussed on my desire and my determination to remain faithful.

For Saint Teresa, there is but one reason for setting out on this journey: union with God's will.

> The whole aim of any person who is beginning prayer - and don't forget this, because it's very important - should be that he work and prepare himself with determination and every possible effort to bring his will into conformity with God's will (II,1:8).

Clearly, this truth extends far beyond the beginnings of the spiritual life, for "the greatest perfection attainable along the spiritual path lies in this conformity. It is the person who lives in more perfect conformity who will receive more from the Lord and be more advanced on this road" (*ibid.*). This is perfection: to be completely one with God's will. Such union is exemplified in the life and teaching of Jesus. Therefore, "don't think that in what concerns perfection there is some mystery or things unknown or still to be understood, for in perfect conformity to God's will lies all our good" (*ibid.*). And Jesus has established the standard for such conformity. Fidelity to prayer and consistency in the determination to progress in the spiritual life are primary means for growing toward union with God's will.

Even with this affirmation and awareness, my failures are disheartening and once again raise the specter of questioning the value of the entire process. "If you should at times fall don't become discouraged and stop striving to advance. For even from this fall God will draw out good" (II,1:9). Constantly, I must remind myself that God's grace can transform all things into my benefit for the spiritual journey if I am determined to strive for fidelity.

> Provided that we don't give up, the Lord will guide everything for our benefit, even though we may not find someone to teach us. There is no remedy for this evil of giving up prayer than to begin again; otherwise the soul will gradually lose more each day - and please God that it will understand this fact (II,1:10).

RELATIONSHIPS

Relationships with others reflect many of the characteristics cited in the first mansion; yet, there has been some progress. Though I am still somewhat inconsistent in my relationships, I am attracted to specific individuals. To the degree that I am willing to enter into and make some effort to sustain those relationships, I can and do achieve varying levels of unselfishness. Basically, I still would like life to move along according to my plans and preferences, but I am growing in the ability to listen to others' perspectives.

I am especially attracted to those who share my interest in the spiritual life. Those who appear to be more advanced along the pathways of the spiritual journey are helpful and understanding through their suggestions and recommendations for my continued growth. My associations and discussions with them are of genuine support when I am discouraged by my own failures in fidelity and in my determination to maintain attentiveness to the spiritual life.

As my time permits, I do attend an occasional conference or class concerning some religious or spiritual topic, and I have participated in a few retreats. I find that the quality of the church community to which I belong is more important to me now than in the past. The quality and content of the liturgies and homilies are of significant assistance for my spiritual life. I went through a period of "shopping around" for a parish before I discovered one in which I felt comfortable and which addressed my current needs. The people I have met and the relationships I have developed through all these activities have made me aware that I do have companions and acquaintances for the spiritual journey. I am not alone in this process.

Generally speaking, relationships in this second mansion are healthy, though they tend to remain focussed on self-fulfillment and personal benefit. This tendency is more evident in my professional relationships with business associates. It is less evident in those relationships which I perceive as having something to do with my spiritual life.[2] Paralleling the concern about vulnerability before God in prayer, there is a hesitancy in becoming too vulnerable in my encounters and relationships with other people. Initial efforts are made, but my lack of attentiveness to maintenance often undermines those efforts.

Fortunately, there is an openness to the interest and assistance received from spiritual directors and other companions. This openness invites and challenges me to greater trust, to move beyond hesitancy and fear. In both prayer and relationships, I must not "become disconsolate if (I) don't respond at once to the Lord" (II,1:3). Patience and perseverance are significant practices for the present; they must become standard priorities for the future.

DETERMINATION

Second mansion dwellers are more sensitive and receptive to all dimensions of life than those in the first mansion. They are developing their awareness of the need for conformity to God's will and, therefore, are making sincere efforts to deepen that awareness through a variety of spiritual practices. Those efforts, however, are not sustained with any consistency. Precisely because those in the second mansion desire to grow in the spiritual life, they tend to become discouraged by their inconsistencies and failures in this regard. Fortunately, their resources now include spiritual directors and other individuals who can assist and encourage them to continue the journey.

Those in the second mansion are growing in

---

[2]. All relationships, of course - personal, professional, "spiritual" - affect and are affected by the spiritual life. Second mansion dwellers compartmentalize their life and so do not immediately see the connections and interdependence necessarily present among the different dimensions of life.

their determination to remain faithful, to put their desires into practice. They are even willing to take up some "penitential practices, for the soul that enters this dwelling place always begins wanting to practice some penance" (II,1:3). However, their determination is not yet solid enough to have a definitive influence on their life style. Thus, growth comes only slowly through the cycle of efforts, failures, and renewed efforts.

The experiences of the second mansion also include a keener sense of the presence and power of evil. Those in this mansion know they must struggle against the evils which can lead them away from the pathways of the spiritual journey. Particularly in this are they aware of the need for a stable determination to maintain their efforts toward continuity and consistency in that journey.

> Certainly the soul undergoes great trials here. If the devil, especially, realizes that (this soul) has all it needs in its temperament and habits to advance far, he will gather all hell together to make the soul go back outside (II,1:5).

Nevertheless, if we continue our efforts, God's grace will support us precisely so we will not "suffer deception and give up what was begun" (II,1:6).

With determination we can and will continue the journey. Saint Teresa's advice at this point is most wise:

> Let them trust in the mercy of God and not at all in themselves, and they will see how His Majesty brings them from the dwelling places of one stage to those of another...And they shall enjoy many more blessings than one can desire - blessings even in this life, I mean (II,1:9).

Thus, we have come to the doorway of the third mansion.

"THERE ARE MANY OF THESE SOULS IN THE WORLD"

THIRD MANSION

"There are many of these souls in the world." This is, indeed, an encouraging statement. It is evidence that those who persevere do progress yet deeper into the castle, steadily moving closer to the innermost chambers where God dwells. Fidelity to what has gone before and the efforts to resist turning back are essential components for entering the third mansion.

> Here you will see how important it was to win the previous battles. I am certain the Lord never fails to give a person like this security of conscience, which is no small blessing. I said "security" and I was wrong, for there is no security in this life; so always understand that I mean "if he doesn't abandon the path he began on" (III,1:1).

And, provided we continue making the efforts necessary to remain on this path, "there is no reason why entrance even into the final dwelling place should be denied these souls, nor will the Lord deny them this entrance if they desire it" (III,1:5). This is encouraging indeed!

The work yet involved to remain faithful and to continue the journey into the castle characterizes this as the mansion of self-renunciation. To nurture our desire for the Lord, to facilitate our continuing forward movement on this journey in cooperation with God's grace, we must lay aside and avoid whatever could hinder our progress and our attentiveness to the Lord.

SELF-RENUNCIATION

"What shall we say to those who through perseverance and the mercy of God have won these battles and have entered the rooms of the third stage, if not: *Blessed is the man who fears the Lord*?" (III,1:1). Our fidelity and perseverance interacting with and responding to God's ever-present and ever-active grace and mercy constitute the door to this third mansion. Thus Saint Teresa of Avila emphasizes how important it is for third mansion dwellers to recognize that "the Lord has done them no small favor, but a very great one, in letting them get through the first difficulties" (III,1:5). Truly, this is a great blessing.

To continue the growth we have experienced thus far in our journey through the first two mansions, "there is need of still more in order that the soul possess the Lord completely, it is not enough to say we want it" (III,1:6). Clearly, we must move beyond desire. We must act upon what we want and make the efforts necessary to achieve it. It is characteristic of third mansion dwellers to take quite seriously their growth in the spiritual life.

> They long not to offend His Majesty, even guarding themselves against venial sins; they are fond of doing penance and setting aside periods for recollection; they spend their time well, practicing works of charity toward their neighbors; and are very balanced in their use of speech and dress and in the governing of their households (III,1:5).

It is not surprising, then, to hear Teresa exclaim, "Certainly, this is a state to be desired" (*ibid.*). Certainly!

Within the experience of the third mansion our approach to the spiritual life becomes more disciplined and organized than it has been thus far. As Saint Teresa has indicated above, third mansion dwellers "are fond of doing penance." A few paragraphs later she expands on this. "The penance these souls do is well balanced, like their lives. They desire penance a great deal so as to serve our Lord by it. Nothing of this is wrong, and thus they are very discreet in doing it in a way so as not to harm their health" (III,2:7). Thus, the mortifications adopted in the third mansion are realistic and untouched by the extremism which can sometimes mark those ascetical practices taken up in the second mansion. In fact, these mortifications could be described as tempered since third mansion dwellers are concerned about their health. So much is this concern in evidence that Teresa is compelled to say, "worry over our health will not improve our health. This I know. And I also know that the whole affair doesn't lie in what pertains to the body, for this is what is the least important" (III,2:8).

In addition, our approach to the spiritual life is more organized. We use our time and possessions well, and we are balanced in dealing with everyday life. We have a sense of control over our spiritual life and we cherish that. We are aware of our weaknesses and limitations, yet we see that there is a direction, a movement in what we are doing. As can be seen, those in the third mansion have achieved a level of integration in the spiritual life which gives them some insight and natural qualities for leadership among those along the initial pathways of the spiritual journey.

The principal challenge confronting us in the third mansion is the need to keep moving. We have a feeling of accomplished progress in this mansion; the temptation will be to stay where we are precisely because this mansion is an excellent one. Even though, as will be seen, we do experience some dryness in our prayer and judgmentalism in our relationships, still, "since we are so circumspect, everything offends us because we fear everything; so we don't dare go further - as if we could reach these dwelling places while leaving to other persons the trouble of treading the path for us" (III,2:8). Teresa explains that humility is the key to continued progress.

With humility present, this stage is a most excellent one. If humility is lacking, we will remain here our whole life - and with a thousand afflictions and miseries. For since we will not have abandoned ourselves, this state will be very laborious and burdensome (III,2:9).

It is possible, then, to "get stuck" in this third mansion. Since things are going well generally, and since we have a sense of our progress, we can become hesitant and less willing to move forward. From Saint Teresa's perspective, this is a lack of humility and trust; ultimately, it is a form of pride and arrogance. This possibility of getting stuck is the shadow side of the reality that "there are many of these souls in the world" (III,1:5). Self-renunciation is necessary here.

PRAYER

As Saint Teresa noted, third mansion dwellers are accustomed to "setting aside periods for recollection" (III,1:5). My prayer could be described as active recollection. I began this way of praying during my sojourn in the previous mansion. Now I have developed a facility for maintaining my focus and attention on the Lord through discursive meditation. As a stimulant, I often use the scriptures, or readings from the Liturgy, or stories from the life of Jesus or one of the saints, or a psalm or antiphon from the Liturgy of the Hours.

I do sense that I have grown and am growing in the spiritual life. I have been able to introduce some others to mental prayer since, like me, they had been searching for further discipline and organization in their spiritual life and practices. From time to time I have even been asked to speak to some groups due to my interest in the spiritual life.

However, even with all this progress that I have

made thus far, I do experience dryness in prayer from time to time. Though I do not neglect prayer, nothing seems to happen during these dry periods. Even when I choose my favorite scripture text or story, it seems but ink on the paper. I find such experiences to be curious and unsettling. They are curious because they come unannounced. I would be able to understand them if I had changed my approach to prayer dramatically and immediately prior to these experiences. But this is not the case. And, these experiences are unsettling since I cannot explain them and really do not believe they should be happening at all. It is disturbing that I do not have some control over this aspect of my spiritual life. It seems that I should be able to work on this, but I also wonder if I can do that with my own resources.

When Saint Teresa comments on this attitude of complaining about dryness, she implies that a lack of humility lies at the root.

> After these years, when it seems they have become lords of the world, at least clearly disillusioned in its regard, His Majesty will try them in some minor matters, and they will go about so disturbed and afflicted that it puzzles me and even makes me fearful. It's useless to give them advice, for since they have engaged so long in the practice of virtue they think they can teach others and that they are more than justified in feeling disturbed (III,2:1).

The humble learning which must yet come is the conviction that "you have not put our Lord under any obligation to grant you these kinds of favors. Rather, as one who has received more, you are more indebted" (III,1:8). But, this is never easy precisely because "we are fonder of consolations than we are of the cross" (III,1:9).

Through the dryness and other crosses I occasionally experience in prayer and daily life, I am learning more about my own weakness and about my need to depend on God. A fault I can see in myself is that when my prayer goes well I tend to credit myself with responsibility for this progress in the spiritual journey. Even though I do not like them, dryness and the cross are, in fact, strengthening my self-knowledge and, I believe, leading me toward greater humility.

> Be convinced that where humility is truly present God will give a peace and conformity - even though He may never give consolations - by which one will walk with greater contentment than will others with their consolations...Test us, Lord - for you know the truth - so that we may know ourselves (*ibid.*).

RELATIONSHIPS

I am a good friend, commitment and loyalty are important to me in maintaining relationships. I enjoy spending time with my friends, working on projects with them, buying an occasional gift for them, helping and supporting them as much as I can. I want them to see my "best" side because I believe that will benefit those relationships. I am pleased with what I am able to do for and with my friends. And I am happy they are my friends, especially since they seem to be a good bit like me.

Beyond what I do for my friends, I feel myself called to some type of service for others and I try to respond as my time permits. "Practicing charity toward (my) neighbors" (III,1:5) has a new importance to me and I am willing to share my time and possessions as feasible. If my assistance can, in some way, enhance their quality of life, then I have done some good. In the process, I may even be able to teach them something about their spiritual journey.

Saint Teresa does note that there is a shadow side in all this. Third mansion dwellers have a tendency to re-create everyone in their own image and likeness. This need not always be explicit; it often exists only within their thoughts or judgments of others, but it can be communicated more directly through suggestions and recommendations which are offered to others. For third mansion dwellers, their way of approaching and accomplishing everything becomes the standard against which everyone is judged. They are distressed when considering the many faults of others and can even imagine that their distress is for the good of others.

> They would like everyone to live a life as well ordered as they do; and please God they will not think their grief is for the faults of others and in their minds turn it into something meritorious (III,2:5).

I am disappointed and even a bit shocked when I see the faults of others. I often wish I could do something to lead them away from their weaknesses toward a better way of living. I believe I could teach them a great deal.

Saint Teresa presents a significant challenge in response to this line of thinking, a challenge solidly grounded in humility.

> Let us look at our own faults and leave aside those of others, for it is very characteristic of persons with such well-ordered lives to be shocked by everything. Perhaps we could truly learn from the one who shocks us what is most important even though we may surpass him in external composure and our way of dealing with others. Although good, these latter things are not what is most important; nor is there any reason to desire that everyone follow at once our own path, or to set about teaching the way of the spirit to someone who perhaps doesn't know what such a thing is. For with these desires that God gives us, about the good of souls, we can make many mistakes (III,2:13).

Third mansion dwellers can be of genuine support in their relationships with others. Still, this does not automatically certify them as competent spiritual directors, though they can appear as such to first and second mansion dwellers. In offering support, those in this third mansion must not forget their own faults and their own need for God's grace at work within them.

OBEDIENCE

Those in the third mansion have benefitted greatly from God's mercy and from their own perseverance in the spiritual life. They are doing well and are serious about continuing the spiritual journey. However, they must be cautioned from time to time not to take themselves so seriously as to believe and expect that all the pathways still before them on the spiritual journey will be open, easy, and smooth.

> Since these souls realize that they wouldn't commit a sin for anything - many wouldn't even advertently commit a venial sin - and that they conduct their lives and households well, they cannot accept patiently that the door of entry to the place where our King dwells be closed to them who consider themselves His vassals (III,1:6).

Even with as far as they have come and as much as they have done, third mansion dwellers must embrace the reality that more of the journey lies ahead. There are other doors in the castle yet to be opened. Patience and humility are essential.

A common mistake among third mansion dwellers is to establish the consolations they experience in prayer and their way of doing things in daily life as the certain standards for sure progress in the spiritual life. It is precisely those standards which must be renounced during the sojourn through this mansion. Clearly, there is a genuine fear about doing this since third mansion dwellers sense they will lose control over their well-ordered lives and thus be left with nothing to show for all their efforts in the spiritual journey.

Saint Teresa of Avila insists here, and throughout the *Interior Castle*, that "the journey I am speaking of must be taken with great humility" (III,2:8). Near the end of her presentation of this third mansion, Teresa gives us an insight into the means for continuing this journey in humility.

> What it seems to me would be highly beneficial for those who through the goodness of the Lord are in this state (for, as I have said, He grants them no small mercy because they are very close to ascending higher) is that they study diligently how to be prompt in obedience...It would a great thing for them to have - as do many persons - someone whom they could consult so as not to do their own will in anything. Doing our own will is usually what harms us (III,2:12).

This is an important directive: consult a spiritual director, a soul mate, whose advice is trustworthy. The importance of this for third mansion dwellers is simple and direct: "Since they are close to the first dwelling places, they could easily return to them" (*ibid.*).

Obedience, of course, includes but goes far beyond any relationship with a spiritual director or soul mate. Something more pervasive is called for here. Obedience is made evident "in striving to practice the virtues, in surrendering our will to God in everything, in bringing our life into accordance with what His Majesty ordains for it, and in desiring that His will not ours be done" (III,2:6). This posture of humility, this response of obedience to God's will, leads us to the doorway of the fourth mansion.

"THE LORD GIVES WHEN HE DESIRES"

FOURTH MANSION

"The Lord gives when He desires." We could infer from this statement that the fourth mansion is a point of receiving gifts from the Lord, as the Lord wishes. Such an inference is quite accurate for, Saint Teresa explains, "supernatural experiences begin here" (IV,1:1). Now we enter the mystical or passive parts of the spiritual life which extend through the remaining mansions. The fourth mansion is the point of both beginning and transition.

The first three mansions constituted the natural or active parts of our spiritual journey. Our growth within and through those mansions, though surely the work of God's grace, depended very much upon the time and energy and effort we were willing to dedicate to the self-knowledge, desire, and self-renunciation characterizing those mansions. We were, in a sense, the primary source of activity in the first, second, and third mansions. This is why Teresa says "there is no certain rule" (IV,1:2) regarding the amount of time we spend in those mansions; it will vary from person to person.

The fourth mansion provides our introduction to those dimensions of the spiritual journey in which the Lord will be the primary source of activity. The passivity implicit in this does not mean that we are excused from any further responsibility for our continuing spiritual growth and development. It refers, rather, to the fact that we cannot generate the experiences of which Saint Teresa will speak in the remaining mansions.

The prayer and the posture necessary for this transition and for openness to receive the Lord's graces in these dwelling places of the castle, characterize this as the mansion of quiet. The gift of quiet fixes our attention on the Lord; indeed, we must completely attentive, "for the Lord gives when He desires, as He desires, and to whom He desires" (IV,1:2).

QUIET

Even with the wisdom and spiritual maturity which Teresa of Avila possessed by the time she was writing the *Interior Castle*, still, she is well aware of the challenge involved in trying to explain super-natural experiences.

> In order to begin to speak of the fourth dwelling place I really need to entrust myself, as I've already done, to the Holy Spirit and beg Him to speak for me from here on that I may say something about the remaining rooms in a way that you will understand. For supernatural experiences begin here. These are something most difficult to explain (IV,1:1).

The door to this mansion is the gift of the prayer of quiet. Technically, this is called infused recollection. Saint Teresa explains.

> Don't think this recollection is acquired by the intellect striving to think about God within itself, or by the imagination imagining Him within itself. Such efforts are good and an excellent kind of meditation because they are founded on a truth, which is that God is within us. But this isn't the prayer of recollection because it is something each one can do - with the help of God... But what I'm speaking of comes in a different way... One noticeably senses a gentle drawing inward... In the case of this recollection, it doesn't come when we want it but when God wants to grant us the favor (IV,3:3).

Several important points can be drawn from this text. First, Teresa distinguishes the prayer of quiet from the simple recollection begun in the second mansion. Quiet, or infused recollection, does not result from the work of our intellect or imagination; it is a gift. Second, this does not negate or diminish the value of our prayer forms during the previous mansions. Their goodness and value rest firmly upon the truth that God dwells within us. Third, the experience of quiet involves a sense of being drawn inward to focus on the Lord, as distinct from earlier experiences of prayer in which we turned inward to focus our attention on the Lord. Fourth, we do not determine when to enter the prayer of quiet; that remains God's determination since this prayer is within the supernatural part of the spiritual life.

The growth and development we experienced in the first three mansions are reflected in all this; nevertheless, they do not cause it. Rather, that growth and development have been but preparations, gradually opening us to accept the gifts which God grants in the fourth mansion. Thus, quiet is both a prayer and a posture of receptivity to the Lord; indeed, it is a way of life which "strives to remain attentive and aware of what the Lord is working in it" (IV,3:4).

The profile of those to whom the Lord grants the gift of quiet is clearly consistent with the progress made in the first three mansions.

> I for myself hold that when His Majesty grants it, He does so to persons who are already beginning to despise the things of the world... So I believe that if we desire to make room for His Majesty, He will give not only this but more, and give it to those whom He begins to call to advance further (IV,3:3).

Fourth mansion dwellers experience that God is becoming the focus of life, the reason for life, and the meaning in life. Materialism and related attitudes have much less influence upon our life than before; our identity is becoming more firmly rooted in the Lord alone.

The principal challenge confronting us in the fourth mansion - and in the remaining mansions as well - is the need to accept the truth that we cannot generate these experiences on our own. They ever remain gifts from God to which we must be receptive. Fidelity to prayer is imperative. Because infused recollection is a gift, we do not therefore abandon our prayer; this would seriously disrupt our relationship with the Lord. Saint Teresa is explicit on this.

> I am very afraid that this will happen to anyone to whom God has granted this favor and who withdraws from prayer - unless he does so for a particularly special reason - or if he doesn't return quickly to prayer, for he will go from bad to worse. I know there is a great deal to fear in this matter (IV,3:10).

The Lord's gifts possess the inherent quality of enabling us to receive them. Our activities, then, in themselves, do not block God's gifts; it is our will which opens or closes us to those gifts. In this fourth mansion, as we are drawn into the supernatural dimensions of the spiritual life, we are given the graces necessary to be sensitive and receptive to God's gifts. We must be open to those gifts, acknowledge them, accept them, and allow them to lead us ever more deeply into the castle.

PRAYER

Before commenting on prayer in the fourth mansion, one preliminary remark is important for readers of the *Interior Castle*. Possibly because she is speaking of a transitional period, Saint Teresa is not always consistent and clear in distinguishing between simple recollection and the prayer of quiet or infused recollection. To make matters even more cloudy, she also speaks of "consolations" and "spiritual delights." So, while reading Teresa, it is helpful to recall that simple recollection and consolations result from our own efforts in response to God's grace. Infused recollection (quiet) and spiritual delights are purely God's work within us.

> Since His Majesty desires to do so - when He is pleased to grant some supernatural favor - He produces this delight with the greatest peace and quiet and sweetness in the very interior part of ourselves. I don't know from where or how, nor is that happiness and delight experienced, as are earthly consolations, in the heart (IV,2:4) This spiritual delight is not something that can be imagined, because however diligent our efforts we cannot acquire it (IV,2:6).

Prayer in the fourth mansion is a point of convergence between the natural and supernatural dimensions of the spiritual life. This convergence is necessary so we can be drawn by the Lord's gifts through the transition from natural to supernatural. Because much has been said already in the preceding section about the nature of the prayer of quiet which characterizes this mansion, extensive additions will not be made here. Rather, two related points will be highlighted.

First, I would like to be able to say that I have no distractions in prayer, but that is definitely not the case. Sometimes, like Teresa, "it seems as if there are in my head many rushing rivers and that these waters are hurtling downward, and many little birds and whistling sounds" (IV,1:9). I do not physically hear any of this of course, but it is sufficiently distracting to discourage me from time to time, making me wonder if I am making any progress or if I am simply fooling myself. The temptation is to abandon prayer altogether.

I equated growth in prayer with ease and with the lack of any disruptive elements. Now I am learning that this is not necessarily the case. In fact, as Saint Teresa notes,

Just as we cannot stop the movement of the heavens, but they proceed in rapid motion, so neither can we stop our mind; and then the faculties of the soul go with it, and we think we are lost and have wasted the time spent before God. But the soul is perhaps completely joined with Him in the dwelling places very close to the center while the mind is on the outskirts of the castle suffering from a thousand wild and poisonous beasts, and meriting by this suffering. As a result we should not be disturbed; nor should we abandon prayer (IV,1:9).

There is a very important lesson here. Distractions in prayer do not automatically signal a lack of growth in prayer. And, by way of parallel, growth in prayer does not necessarily include a complete cessation of distractions.

At the root of all this is the continuing need to grow in self-knowledge. "Terrible trials are suffered because we don't understand ourselves, and that which isn't bad at all but good we think is a serious fault... For the most part all the trials and disturbances come from our not understanding ourselves" (*ibid.*). At this point in the spiritual journey, self-knowledge teaches me that the natural abilities of the mind - and the body - are not, in themselves, disruptive of spiritual growth. How I interpret them and what I choose to do in response to them may disrupt my continuing development. So, when distractions come, "it would be very bad if I were to abandon everything on account of this obstacle" (IV,1:11).

Second, it is much clearer to me now than in the past that the true gauge of prayer is not so much what happens during prayer as how it affects my behaviors in everyday life. Obviously, prayer is significant 'in facilitating that "the will must in some way be united with God's will. But it is in the effects and deeds following afterward that one discerns the true value in prayer; there is no better crucible for testing prayer" (IV,2:8).

The most profound effects and the most productive deeds are those which reflect the transforming power of love. Through prayer I can be drawn ever deeper into union with God who is love. Increasingly, then, love should mark every aspect of my life. Living this love will be the means by which the Lord will guide me to the remaining mansions.

> I only wish to inform you that in order to profit by this path and ascend to the dwelling places we desire, the important thing is not to think much but to love much; and so do that which best stirs you to love. Perhaps we don't know what love is. I wouldn't be very surprised, because it doesn't consist in great delight but in desiring with strong determination to please God in everything, in striving, insofar as possible, not to offend Him, and in asking Him for the advancement of the honor and glory of His Son and the increase of the Catholic Church. These are the signs of love (IV,1:7).

These are the signs as well of growth in prayer, for this fourth mansion and for those remaining.

RELATIONSHIPS

As there is less possessiveness of material things in this mansion, so too, there are fewer tendencies to dominate others, to possess them, as a support for personal identity. I am growing in my ability to allow others to be themselves, without needing to re-fashion them to suit me. My relationships with others, in many ways, reflect my relationship with the Lord. I realize the Lord is "other," a giver of gifts whom I do not control. Similarly, I recognize the people I encounter every day as "other;" they are not merely extensions of myself. As I often need to be still - interiorly and exteriorly - before the Lord, to listen and to learn, so too I need to look and to see others as they are.

I make the efforts to serve others, to be as generous as possible. I experience a great desire to place myself at the disposal of others. As Saint Teresa says, "the soul is not as tied down as it was before in things pertaining to the service of God, but has much more freedom" (IV,3:9). Of course, trials and difficulties occasionally accompany service to others, but I simply accept these realities as inevitable parts of life.

> The fear the soul used to have of trials and losing its health has disappeared, and it now thinks it will be able to do all things in God and has greater desire for penance than previously. The fear it used to have of trials it now sees to be tempered. Its faith is more alive; it knows that if it suffers trials for God, His Majesty will give it the grace to suffer them with patience. Sometimes it even desires them because there also remains a strong will to do something for God (*ibid.*).

I know and experience that I do have an influence upon others. They express an interest in my insights and perspectives concerning the spiritual life, and in my experiences of prayer. Some even have asked about my willingness to serve as a spiritual director, to help and lead them in prayer. I do sense that I can lead others to prayer and I believe this can do some good in supporting them on their spiritual journey. In fact, Teresa acknowledges that "such a soul can do a great deal of harm to the devil by getting others to follow it, and it could be of great benefit to God's Church" (IV,3:10).

I realize the responsibility involved in this, which is precisely why fidelity to prayer and attentiveness to spiritual growth are very high priorities for me. I am keenly aware that Saint Teresa's sobering comment about fourth mansion dwellers is applicable to me: "If they go astray, they stray much more than do others" (*ibid.*).

ATTENTIVENESS

Since this is a time of transition, fourth mansion dwellers must be especially attentive to the Lord's subtle movements, inviting them to yet deeper levels within the castle. This is a challenge because our journey and experiences through the first three mansions have accustomed us to acting and doing and making efforts. Now we must fix our attention on what God is doing in our life, on the direction in which we are being called. Our attentiveness to the Lord's activity, our patience in listening for the Lord's call, and our willingness in following the Lord's lead are means through which we will be guided by God's grace toward the central room of the castle.

This attentiveness must extend, likewise, to our openness for receiving the gift of the prayer of quiet. Even though quiet is a gift, we can dispose ourselves to receive it. Saint Teresa offers encouragement in this regard. "It is good to try to understand how we can obtain such a favor; so I am going to tell you what I have understood about this" (IV,2:8). Nothing can be said about the timing of this gift; there is no general rule concerning when we will receive quiet precisely because "it is given only to whom God wills to give it and often when the soul is least thinking of it" (IV,2:9). Thus, Teresa's recommendation for disposing ourselves to receive this gift is simple and direct.

> After you have done what should be done by those in the previous dwelling places: humility! humility! By this means the Lord allows Himself to be conquered with regard to anything we want from Him. The first sign for seeing whether or not you have humility is that you do not think you deserve these favors and spiritual delights from the Lord or that you will receive them in your lifetime (*ibid.*).

Thus disposed, we will be able to find support to sustain our attentiveness in the midst of the experiences which flow from the gifts we receive. We can receive support from our spiritual director, but also from others within the fourth mansion, for Saint Teresa clearly gives the impression that it is a well-populated place. "I have greatly enlarged upon this dwelling place because it is the one which more souls enter" (IV,3:14). The Lord is not sparing in granting this gift of quiet or infused recollection. It is necessary, however, that we recognize this gift when it comes.

Having been brought by the Lord into the supernatural parts of the spiritual life through our experiences in the fourth mansion, now we must remain constant as we continue to receive God's gifts. We "must persevere in receiving them, for in this perseverance lies all our good" (IV,3:9). It is most wise and prudent, then, to accept Teresa's advice at this point.

> May whoever experiences this within himself praise God greatly because it is indeed right to recognize the favor and give thanks, for doing so will dispose one for other greater favors (IV,3:4).

Thus, we await the Lord's invitation to enter the fifth mansion.

"HOW CAN I EXPLAIN THE RICHES AND TREASURES AND DELIGHTS"

FIFTH MANSION

"How can I explain the riches and treasures and delights." This is precisely the challenge confronting Saint Teresa of Avila as she opens her reflections on the fifth mansion. The challenge will become no less formidable as she proceeds to explain the remaining mansions which are deep within the supernatural part of the spiritual life. As she says,

> How can I explain the riches and treasures and delights found in the fifth dwelling places? I believe it would be better not to say anything about these remaining rooms, for there is no way of knowing how to speak about them; neither is the intellect capable of understanding them nor can comparisons help in explaining them; earthly things are too coarse for such a purpose (V,1:1).

Fortunately, Teresa does choose to say something about the remaining rooms. And, as before, she entrusts herself to the Lord in taking up the challenge. "Send light from heaven, Lord, that I might be able to enlighten these Your servants - for You have been pleased that some of them ordinarily enjoy these delights" (*ibid.*).

As with the preceding mansion, we will find ample company in this one, though not all will have the same experiences in the fifth mansion.

> There are indeed only a few who fail to enter this dwelling place of which I shall now speak. There are various degrees, and for that reason I say that most enter these places. But I believe that only a few will experience some of the things that I will say are in this room. Yet even if souls do no more than reach the door, God is being very merciful to them; although many are called few are chosen (V,1:2).

The experiences with which we now are gifted by the Lord characterize this as the mansion of union. It is both more intense and more complete than the partial union we experienced in the fourth mansion through the prayer of quiet. In fact, "this union is above all earthly joys, above all delights, above all consolations, and still more than that" (V,1:6). Thus, as we begin to explore these fifth dwellings places, Saint Teresa recommends,

> since in some way we can enjoy heaven on earth, be brave in begging the Lord to give us His grace in such a way that nothing will be lacking through our own fault; that He show us the way and strengthen the soul that it may dig until it finds this hidden treasure. The truth is that the treasure lies within our very selves (V,1:2).

UNION

The door to this mansion is the gift of the prayer of union. In technical terms, this is called infused contemplation; Teresa describes it as a suspension of the faculties.[1] Before examining the experience of this prayer in the following section, it will be helpful here to comment on what we are called by the Lord to do at this point in our spiritual journey. To illustrate what is happening within our spiritual life in the fifth mansion, Saint Teresa uses two analogies to assist readers in understanding God's gifts and secret communications.

In chapter two of this mansion Teresa introduces the analogy of the silkworm. Though acknowledg-

---

[1]. The "faculties" include our five physical senses and our four spiritual senses of imagination, memory, intellect, and will. "Suspension" refers to their uselessness as channels of communication during the prayer of union. "God wants to enter the center of the soul without going through any door" (V,1:12).

ing she has never seen the process, she provides a basic outline of it. Silkworms nourish themselves and sustain life by feeding on available leaves. Then,

> having grown to full size, they settle on some twigs. There with their little mouths they themselves go about spinning the silk and making some very thick little cocoons in which they enclose themselves. The silkworm, which is fat and ugly, then dies, and a little white butterfly, which is very pretty, comes forth from the cocoon (V,2:2).

Clearly, the analogy is paschal with its emphasis on dying and rising to new life. To assure that this parallel will not be overlooked, Saint Teresa explains, "it begins to spin the silk and build the house wherein it will die. I would like to point out here that this house is Christ" (V,2:4). Our "cocoon" is God; the prayer of union graces us with this intimacy which leads to transformation.

> His Majesty Himself, as He does in this prayer of union, becomes the dwelling place we build for ourselves. It seems I'm saying that we can build up God and take Him away since I say that He is the dwelling place and we ourselves can build it so as to place ourselves in it. And, indeed, we can! Not that we can take God away or build Him up, but we can take away from ourselves and build up, as do these little silkworms (V,2:5).

To experience fully the paschal mystery of God, we must place ourselves deep within God, for this mystery cannot be understood by observation. Like Jesus himself, we must be full participants in the process of dying and rising to new life. Like the silkworm, what we are must die so that what we become can rise to life in union with God. Our identity must be born anew in God. Teresa's advice is urgent.

> Let's be quick to do this work and weave this little cocoon by getting rid of our self-love and self-will, our

attachment to any earthly thing, and by performing deeds of penance, prayer, mortification, obedience, and of all the other things you know...Let it die; let this silkworm die, as it does in completing what it was created to do! (V,2:6).

In chapter four of this mansion Saint Teresa introduces a second analogy. "Even though the comparison may be a coarse one I cannot find another that would better explain what I mean than the sacrament of marriage" (V,4:3). Teresa retains this comparison through the remaining two mansions since it lends itself to the progression which characterizes the spiritual journey. In sixteenth-century Spain the celebration of a marriage was preceded by several stages of varying lengths depending upon the couple's developing affection for one another.[2] Teresa incorporates those stages into her explanation of union.

Here below when two people are to be engaged, there is discussion about whether they are alike, whether they love each other, and whether they might meet together so as to become more satisfied with each other. So, too, in the case of this union with God, the agreement has been made, and this soul is well informed about the goodness of her Spouse and determined to do His will in everything and in as many ways as she sees might make Him happy. And His Majesty, as one who understands clearly whether these things about His betrothed are so, is happy with her (V,4:4).

"It seems to me that the prayer of union does not yet reach the stage of spiritual betrothal" (*ibid*.). Rather, union is precisely that stage in which the potential spouses can come to know one another on

---

[2]. Marriage arrangements included the following: 1- initial meetings; 2 - exchanging gifts; 3 - falling in love; 4 - joining hands; 5 - betrothal; 6 - marriage.

deeper levels. God "grants this mercy, for He desired her to know Him more and that they might meet together...and be united" (*ibid.*). As for the betrothal, it "belongs to the dwelling place we shall speak of after this one" (V,4:5).

The principal challenge confronting us in the fifth mansion is not to be overwhelmed by frustration in discovering that we cannot explain or understand the experience of union. Our "whole intellect would want to be occupied in understanding something of what is felt"; but what we fail to realize is that "the soul does not have the energy to attain to this" (V,1:4). We must accept this as God's work which lies beyond our comprehension. "In regard to all these favors we have to give up looking for reasons to see how they've come about" (V,1:11).

Union, then, reflects an intimacy beyond anything experienced in the first four mansions. God's communications take place deep within the soul, by-passing the faculties; "for it is all a matter of love united with love" (V,4:3).

PRAYER

Prayer in the fifth mansion is not so much a state as it is a brief experience which may happen only once in a lifetime. By the gift of this prayer, God brings the soul to a union more whole than that experienced in the fourth mansion; in fact, "the difference between union and the previous experience is great" (V,1:7). Teresa explains this as a suspension of the faculties.

> There is no need here to use any technique to suspend the mind since all the faculties are asleep in this state - and truly asleep - to the things of the world and to ourselves. As a matter of fact, during the time that the union lasts the soul is left as though without its senses, for it has no power to think even if it wants

to....In sum, it is like one who in every respect has died to the world so as to live more completely in God (V,1:4).

I find there are very few words which adequately describe this experience. I do know that I did nothing which could be considered a cause of this. My prayer immediately prior to that experience was simply the stillness I have known and practiced since the fourth mansion. But I know that something very different took place. Saint Teresa sheds some light on this by identifying "a clear sign by which you will be sure against error or doubts about whether the union is from God" (V,1:7). "During the time of this union the soul neither sees, nor hears, nor understands, because the union is always short and seems to the soul even much shorter than it probably is" (V,1:9). And it was, indeed, a short time; as Teresa notes, "in my opinion the union never lasts for as much as a half hour" (V,2:7).

Even though these descriptions fall short of the experience, I have a definite certitude that I was wholly united to God during that brief period.

> God so places Himself in the interior of the soul that when it returns to itself it can in no way doubt that it was in God and God was in it. This truth remains with it so firmly that even though years go by without God's granting that favor again, the soul can neither forget nor doubt that it was in God and God was in it (V,1:9).

Then, Saint Teresa makes this even stronger.

> I would say that whoever does not receive this certitude does not experience union of the whole soul with God, but union of some faculty, or that he experiences one of the many other kinds of favors God grants souls (V,1:11).

What has been said here cannot be considered generic; that is, applicable to all experiences of

union. Actually, "there are various degrees of intensity" (V,2:1). And, there are many effects[3] of this
prayer which can vary from person to person. The
profound richness of the gift of union is such that
more can always be said about it. "It seems I have
been lengthy, but I could say much more; and who-
ever has received this favor from God will see that
I've been brief" (V,2:9).

RELATIONSHIPS

I can relate to and be united with others on very
deep levels, but I do not place my identity in them.
Though close to and caring of them, I see that we are
distinct and autonomous; I respect their individual-
ity. In my relationships, as in the other dimensions
of my life, I want to maintain my focus on the Lord.
In everything, I "strive to go forward in the service of
our Lord and in self-knowledge" (V,3:1). This service and self-knowledge help me in being attentive to
and conscientious with God's gifts to me.

I believe that the gifts I receive through the
prayer of union have an apostolic quality. I want to
and I enjoy helping others in their efforts to grow
closer to the Lord and to understand the ways of

---

3. To comment on all the effects or benefits which Saint
Teresa cites regarding the prayer of union goes beyond the
scope of these present reflections. Those benefits are elabo-
rated in chapter two, paragraphs 7 to 14. For reference, however, the following list can serve as a summary. Fifth mansion dwellers are characterized by: sense of unworthiness
for this gift; desire to praise the Lord; desire to suffer trials;
desire for penance, solitude, and that all people might know
God; pain on seeing God offended; restlessness because of
longing for God; calm; personal efforts seem insignificant;
less attachment to relatives, friends, wealth; experiences of
the cross; peacefulness.

prayer. That the gifts received in this mansion extend their benefits beyond myself appears to be part of their very nature.

> It is God's desire that a favor so great not be given in vain; if a person doesn't herself benefit, the favor will benefit others. For since the soul is left with these desires and virtues...it always brings profit to other souls during the time that it continues to live virtuously; and they catch fire from its fire...The soul delights in explaining the favors God grants to whoever loves and serves Him (*ibid*.).

Through my relationships, I am called to union with God's will. And I know my shortcomings in those relationships can be a hindrance to that union. Such hindrance comes with "self-love, self-esteem, judging one's neighbors (even though in little things), a lack of charity for them, and not loving them as ourselves" (V,3:6). There is really no mystery to the key for completing God's will, it is as clear as the gospel itself. "The Lord asks of us only two things: love of His Majesty and love of our neighbor. These are what we must work for. By observing them with perfection, we do His will and so will be united with Him" (V,3:7).

I want to love God as Jesus commands, but I have wondered sometimes if it is possible to know that I love God. It is so easy to claim such love without verification. What would be the means for knowing this? Saint Teresa provides an eloquent and definitive response.

> The most certain sign, in my opinion, as to whether or not we are observing these two laws is whether we observe well the love of neighbor. We cannot know whether or not we love God, although there are strong indications for recognizing that we do love Him; but we can know whether we love our neighbor. And be certain that the more advanced you see you are in love for your neighbor the more advanced you will be in the love of God, for the love His Majesty has

for us is so great that to repay us for our love of neighbor He will in a thousand ways increase the love we have for Him. I cannot doubt this (V,3:8).

This sums up what is most essential for all our relationships, "for if we practice love of neighbor with great perfection, we will have done everything" (V,3:9). Such love is inseparable from love of God and so unites us to God's will precisely because it is the living expression of that will.

DILIGENCE

The fifth mansion and the gifts which accompany it are secure, "for there is neither imagination, nor memory, nor intellect that can impede this good" (V,1:5). Temptations are not experienced in our deepest self, though we do encounter the everyday ups and downs of striving to serve and to love others. Saint Teresa goes even further; "I would dare say that if the prayer is truly that of union with God, the devil cannot even enter or do any damage. His Majesty is so joined and united with the essence of the soul that the devil will not dare approach nor will he even know about this secret" (*ibid.*).

Clearly, there is great comfort to be found in such security, in such protection by God. However, this is all the more reason to be diligent; for "in spite of all these benefits the soul is not entirely surrendered to God's will" (V,2:10). The will, our ability to choose and decide, is the most noble of the faculties. It is a power we have by creation and the means through which we reflect and live the image and likeness of God. This is the faculty God wants to possess through union. Saint Teresa uses the image of wax being impressed by a seal to represent what takes places during the prayer of union.

For indeed the soul does no more in this union than does the wax when another impresses a seal on it. The wax doesn't impress the seal upon itself; it is only disposed - I mean by being soft. And even in order to be disposed, it doesn't soften itself but remains still and gives its consent. Oh, the goodness of God...All You want is our will and that there be no impediment in the wax (V,2:12).

Thus the necessity of diligence, because "love is never idle, and a failure to grow would be a very bad sign" (V,4:10). In fact, "works are what the Lord wants!" (V,3:11). In specifying the works necessary to put diligence into practice, Saint Teresa identifies two as the most effective. "First, we must always ask God in prayer to sustain us" (V,4:9). We must maintain our dependence on the Lord for we cannot sustain ourselves in these supernatural parts of the spiritual life. To trust that our own abilities could carry us toward the innermost room of the castle is simply foolish. Second, "we should walk with special care and attention, observing how we are proceeding in the practice of virtue; whether we are getting better or worse in some areas" (*ibid.*). The areas which Teresa mentions are noteworthy: loving others, desiring to be considered the least, performing ordinary tasks. These simple realities are the basic avenues to union with God. Our diligence in them will lead us ever deeper, directly toward that union.

"Let this, in sum, be the conclusion: that we strive always to advance" (V,4:10). Through that striving, we are drawn yet deeper into the castle, even to the entrance of the sixth mansion.

"WHAT INTERIOR AND EXTERIOR TRIALS THE SOUL SUFFERS"

SIXTH MANSION

"What interior and exterior trials the soul suffers." Along the pathways of our spiritual journey, encounters with the cross are more than a possibility, more even than a probability; they are an inevitability. As Saint Teresa observes, "I doubt very much that those persons who sometimes enjoy so truly the things of heaven will live free of earthly trials that come in one way or another" (VI,1:2). There is no new revelation here since this reflects the pattern already traced by Jesus whom we follow and whose name we bear. The experiences of the sixth mansion bring us to the very heart of the paschal mystery, cross and new life. Even as the cross precedes resurrection and complete union with God, "this severe suffering comes so that one may enter the seventh dwelling place" (VI,1:15).

This is the mansion of betrothal. The level of our commitment here is clear and uncompromising.

> Now the soul is fully determined to take no other spouse. But the Spouse does not look at the soul's great desires that the betrothal take place, for He still wants it to desire this more, and He wants the betrothal to take place at a cost; it is the greatest of blessings... Oh, God help me, what interior and exterior trials the soul suffers before entering the seventh dwelling place! (VI,1:1).

Teresa's explanation of the experiences within this mansion constitutes the longest and most complex section of the *Interior Castle*. Even so, Saint Teresa informs us that she will speak of only some sufferings which take place here "because it would be impossible to speak of them all, or even to explain what they are" (VI,1:15). It is also within this mansion that Teresa discusses the extraordinary mystical phenomena which can accompany this stage of the spiritual life. All this is the means by which we are prepared for complete and permanent union with God.

BETROTHAL

Trials and sufferings are the door to this mansion. This is not to imply that no crosses were present in the preceding mansions, only that those encountered in this sixth mansion are of greater intensity. Also, the crosses which appear here are particularly unexpected since they are in such sharp contrast to the relatively pleasant experiences within the fourth and fifth mansions. However intense or unexpected these trials may be, our willingness to embrace them is grounded in the desire to be one with God after the example of Jesus.

The trials and sufferings of which Saint Teresa speaks are not generic. They have a real and definite content which touches us profoundly. As noted earlier, Teresa does not mention all the trials which can be experienced in this mansion. Nevertheless, the ones she does identify provide us with a sufficient profile of the kinds of trials and sufferings which characterize the sixth mansion. Four are cited here. First, "a thousand kinds of ridicule" (VI,1:3). This criticism can reach such a level that we could even begin to fear "that there would be no one who would hear our confession"[1] (VI,1:4). Second, "praise is just another trial greater than those mentioned!" (*ibid*.). Saint Teresa does acknowledge, however, that receiving praise eventually

---

[1]. Saint Teresa herself experienced this. See *Life*, chapter 28, number 14.

becomes tolerable because it highlights that all goodness "is given by His Majesty" (*ibid.*). Third, "the Lord is wont also to send the severest illnesses" (VI,1:6). Even so, Teresa assures us that "God gives no more than what can be endured; and His Majesty gives patience first" (*ibid.*). Fourth, "were we to treat of interior sufferings these others would seem small if the interior ones could be clearly explained; but it is impossible to explain the way in which they come to pass" (VI,1:7). In this, Saint Teresa refers to a variety of interior trials: lack of consolation and understanding, no comfort in our efforts at prayer, advice from scrupulous and inexperienced spiritual directors. The reason for all this is clear: "Our great God wants us to know our own misery and that He is king; and this is very important for what lies ahead" (VI,1:12).

Though there is no way to avoid such crosses, Saint Teresa does provide us with some very practical advice. "The best remedy (I don't mean for getting rid of them, because I don't find any, but so that they may be endured) is to engage in external works of charity and to hope in the mercy of God who never fails those who hope in Him" (VI,1:13).

Beside these encounters with the cross, another characteristic of the sixth mansion is the extraordinary mystical phenomena which can take place. It is beyond the scope of this article to present a full exposition of these; thus, they will be presented in summary form.

The chapters in which Saint Teresa discusses various mystical phenomena are the most extensive part of the sixth mansion and of the *Interior Castle*. Consistent with her flowing style of writing, Teresa does not always separate her comments as she moves from the consideration of one phenomenon to another. Nevertheless, she is clear in insisting upon the supernatural character of these realities.

In this section of the *Interior Castle*, Saint Teresa demonstrates her brilliance; that is, her ability to put into writing realities and truths which are practically incommunicable since they can be truly known only by experience. And even though she speaks of all this from personal experience, Teresa readily admits, "I am struggling, Sisters, to explain for you this action of love, and I don't know how" (VI,2:3).

The first experience - "favor" - which Saint Teresa addresses is the wound of love or, technically, the transverberation of the soul. This is experienced as if the soul had been pierced with an arrow of love.

> This action of love is so powerful that the soul dissolves with desire...It seems this pain reaches to the soul's very depths and that when He who wounds it draws out the arrow, it indeed seems, in accord with the deep love the soul feels, that God is drawing these very depths after Him (VI,2:4).

Thus, a "delightful pain" (*ibid.*) is experienced which facilitates the process of assimilation into God.

Another favor is experienced when God speaks to the soul. "Locutions" are of various kinds. "Some seem to come from outside oneself; others, from deep within the interior part of the soul; others, from the superior part; and some are so exterior that they come through the sense of hearing, for it seems there is a spoken word" (VI,3:1). Saint Teresa alerts us to the necessity of determining the source of locutions since we cannot assume they are always from God. God's words always effect what they say, instill peacefulness, and give certitude about what is said. "All the good comes from how one benefits by these words" (VI,3:4). Teresa writes at length concerning the signs for knowing whether locutions are "from God or from the devil or from one's own imagination...for there are many

souls among prayerful people who hear them"
(*ibid.*).

Raptures are the favor in which the actual
betrothal takes place. The faculties and senses are
suspended so completely that the person may
appear to have fainted. During that time "the Lord
joins the soul with Himself, without anyone understanding what is happening except these two; nor
does the soul itself understand in a way that can
afterward be explained. Yet, it does have interior
understanding" (VI,4:3). Saint Teresa further elab-
orates, "In a rapture, believe me, God carries off for
Himself the entire soul, and, as to someone who is
His own and His spouse, He begins to show it some
little part of the kingdom that it has gained by being
espoused to Him" (VI,4:9).

Another favor given in this mansion is the gift of
profound joy which "makes a person so forgetful of
self and of all things that he doesn't advert to, nor
can he speak of anything other than the praises of
God which proceed from his joy" (VI,6:13). This
favor is "a deep union of the faculties; but our Lord
nonetheless leaves them free that they might enjoy
this joy - and the same goes for the senses - without
understanding what it is they are enjoying or how
they are enjoying" (VI,6:10).

Saint Teresa also explains intellectual and imaginative visions. An intellectual vision "will happen
while the soul is heedless of any thought about such
a favor being granted to it...it will feel Jesus Christ,
our Lord, beside it. Yet, it does not see Him, either
with the eyes of the body or with those of the soul"
(VI,8:2). During an imaginative vision, the Lord

> shows the soul clearly His most sacred humanity
> in the way He desires; either as He was when He went
> about in the world or as He is after His resurrection.
> And even though the vision happens so quickly that
> we could compare it to a streak of lightning, this most
> glorious image remains so engraved on the imagina-

tion that I think it would be impossible to erase it...Although I say "image" let it be understood that, in the opinion of the one who sees it, it is not a painting but truly alive (VI,9:3-4).

Teresa cautions us not to seek these favors. They are gifts given as and when the Lord wills. Seeking them rather than God as their source is a form of pride.

The principal challenge confronting us in the sixth mansion is to avoid equating the reception of these favors with holiness, for "the greater glory is not merited by receiving a large number of these favors; rather, on the contrary, the recipients of these favors are obliged to serve more since they have received more" (VI,9:16). Saint Teresa comments, "there are many holy persons who have never received one of these favors; and others who receive them but are not holy...The soul doesn't think about receiving more but about how to serve for what it has received" (*ibid*.).

These brief comments on the mystical phenomena which can be experienced by sixth mansion dwellers are merely an overview. It is important to read the related sections of the *Interior Castle* for a more complete exposition of Saint Teresa's spiritual teaching, especially since these favors are not given to everyone in a uniform way. In addition, three general points must be kept in mind regarding these favors. First, these phenomena are not "something that can be procured in any human way" (VI,2:4). They are supernatural gifts from God and thus well beyond all human capability and creativity. Second, however sublime these favors, they do not diminish the importance of reflecting on and remaining close to Jesus' humanity. Quite the contrary, "how much more necessary it is not to withdraw through one's own efforts from all our good and help which is the most sacred humanity of our Lord Jesus Christ" (VI,7:6). Third, "our Lord grants these favors to the soul because, as to one to whom He is truly betrothed, one who is already determined to do His will in everything, He desires to give it some knowledge of how to do His will and of His grandeurs" (VI,10:8).

PRAYER

Because much of the material in the preceding section regarding crosses and favors directly concerns the nature and character of prayer in the sixth mansion, the present section will be brief.

My experience of prayer can be described as a convergence of light and darkness. Through the abundance of gifts I receive, I believe I am being drawn toward an increasing intimacy with God. This is a source of joy and light. Yet, at the same time

> the soul doesn't think that it has any love of God or that it ever had any, for if it has done some good, or His Majesty has granted it some favor, all of this seems to have been dreamed up or fancied. As for sins, it sees certainly that it has committed them (VI,1:11).

The more I receive of God's gifts, the more clearly I see the distance between myself and God. Thus my prayer is a burning desire - a longing - to be with God. I wonder sometimes if this longing can ever be fulfilled; still, I have great hope. I experience, as Saint Teresa writes, that the soul

> feels a strange solitude because no creature in all the earth provides it company, nor do I believe would any heavenly creature, not being the One whom it loves...The soul sees that it is like a person hanging, who cannot support himself on any earthly thing; nor can it ascend to heaven. On fire with this thirst, it cannot get to the water; and the thirst is not one that is endurable but already at such a point that nothing will take it away. Nor does the soul desire that the

thirst be taken away save by that water of which our Lord spoke to the Samaritan woman (VI,11:5).

I have become incapable of discursive, mental prayer. Yet, I want to be fully attentive to whatever the Lord may ask of me and do within me so I can respond promptly and fully. In speaking of mental prayer at this point, Saint Teresa writes,

> this inability is very common, for the intellect becomes less capable of meditation. I believe the reason must be that since in meditation the whole effort consists in seeking God and that once God is found the soul becomes used to seeking Him again through the work of the will, the soul doesn't want to tire itself by working with the intellect (VI,7:7).

In general, I describe my prayer as passive. It has become much less a matter of doing than of simply being open to whatever is done within me by the Lord. Because of the nature of the crosses I have encountered and the favors I have received, I understand Teresa's insistence that "strong courage is necessary for the one to whom God grants these favors and even faith and confidence and a full surrender to our Lord so that He may do what He wants with the soul" (VI,5:1). And I realize even this is a gift since "it's necessary that He who gives everything give the courage also" (VI,5:12).

RELATIONSHIPS

I am more genuinely empathetic than at any other point in my life. I see others as truly other and am called and willing to embrace them and to be of service to them. That service is a means for me to avoid discouragement when I experience the trials and sufferings which come into my life. Service is also a practical way for me to express my praise and thanksgiving to God for the favors I have received. And, this service is a very concrete way to "satisfy love, and it is love's nature to serve with deeds in a thousand ways. If it could, love would want to discover ways of consuming the soul within itself" (VI, 9:18).

I recognize my own sinfulness and I realize there are a multitude of offenses against God. That recognition and realization compel me to "be ashamed to feel resentment about anything that is said or done against me" (VI,10:3). I want to be transformed by love for it is the only way to live fully in God's image and likeness. As Saint Teresa teaches,

> let us not think we are doing anything by suffering injuries, but we should very eagerly endure everything, and let us love the one who offends us since this great God has not ceased to love us even though we have offended Him very much. Thus the Lord is right in wanting all to pardon the wrongs done to them (VI,10:4).

Relationships - with God and others - in the sixth mansion demand a death to self. In particular, relationships with others must be ever marked by compassion and forgiveness and love. I desire to respond as fully as possible to that demand because this is a principal means for imitating and being united with God who shows me compassion and forgiveness and love.

COURAGE

> All these sufferings are means to increase one's desire to enjoy the Spouse. And His Majesty, as one who knows our weakness, is enabling the soul through these afflictions and many others to have the courage to be joined with so great a Lord and to take Him as its Spouse (VI,4:1).

Courage is necessary for the crosses we encounter and for the favors we receive in the sixth mansion. At first reading, such a statement may strike us as curious. It is understandable that courage will be necessary to bear the crosses we encounter. But, why is courage necessary for receiving the Lord's favors? Precisely because those favors are far beyond the realm of human comprehension and explanation.

> I tell you there is need for more courage than you think. Our nature is very timid and lowly when it comes to something so great, no matter how much you might see that the favor is good for us, it would be impossible for you to receive that favor. And thus you will see what His Majesty does to conclude this betrothal, which I understand comes about when He gives the soul raptures that draw it out of its senses. For if it were to see itself so near this great majesty while in its senses, it would perhaps die (VI,4:2).

When speaking of a particular kind of rapture, Saint Teresa insists, "great courage is necessary, for this favor is something frightening. If our Lord were not to give such courage, the soul would always go about deeply distressed" (VI,5:5).

Courage is also necessary for self-knowledge in the sixth mansion. The crosses and favors encountered here show us clearly that everything in our life is a gift from God. We possess nothing of our own. Thus, we have a keen awareness of our profound poverty and complete dependence upon God.

> How pleased our Lord is that we know ourselves and strive to reflect again and again on our poverty and misery and on how we possess nothing that we have not received...Courage is necessary for this knowledge and for the many other graces given to the soul the Lord has brought to this stage. And when there is humility, courage, in my opinion, is even more necessary for this knowledge of one's own misery (VI,5:6).

This clearly echoes Saint Teresa's teaching in the very first mansion concerning the importance and necessity of self-knowledge throughout the entire spiritual journey. Thus, even for those in the sixth mansion, Teresa prays that "we will be granted the favor never to leave this path of self-knowledge, amen" (VI,10:7).

Courage is necessary to serve God. Because the crosses and favors received in this mansion can have physical and public manifestations, we may be inclined to remain in private to avoid embarrassment and the rash judgment of others. We would thereby interrupt our service to others. Drawing from her own experience, Teresa is quite blunt in commenting on such inclinations.

> It seems to me that this pain and embarrassment amount to a lack of humility, for if this person desires to be reviled, what difference does it make what others think? But the soul cannot control such feelings. One who was in this affliction[2] heard from the Lord: "Don't be afflicted. Either they will praise Me or criticize you; and in either case you gain" (VI,4:16).

Courage will be necessary to remain steadfast in rendering service. Thus, "may it please His Majesty to give us the courage so that we may merit to serve Him, amen" (VI,5:12).

Even as the elements of the paschal mystery are united, so too, the trials and favors in the sixth mansion are intimately related. "Do not think the favors are given continually; rather, for each time the Lord grants them there are many trials" (VI,9:16). Together, these trials and favors draw us deeper into union with God. God's grace of courage will strengthen us for the journey toward the seventh mansion and into the central room of the castle.

The sixth mansion is situated deep within the castle, very close to the seventh mansion. Thus, Teresa observes that "there is no closed door

---

[2]. Saint Teresa is referring to herself.

between the one and the other. Because there are things in the last that are not revealed to those who have not yet reached it, I thought I should divide them" (VI,4:4). And now, through the trials and favors we have received in the sixth mansion, the Lord has prepared us to be escorted into the seventh dwelling place.[3]

---

3. As stated earlier in these reflections, it is important to read Saint Teresa's own descriptions of and commentaries on the experiences of sixth mansion dwellers. Addressing the complexities of this mansion in such brief reflections as these is inevitably incomplete. Thus the importance of reading and reflecting on Teresa's own words.

"LET US CALL IT ANOTHER HEAVEN"

SEVENTH MANSION

"Let us call it another heaven." Saint Teresa opens her presentation of the seventh mansion by noting that her readers may think "it will be impossible for anything more to be said" (VII,1:1). After all, profound and even extraordinary dimensions of the spiritual journey have been revealed already. Teresa dismisses such thinking as foolish and asks, "who will finish telling of God's mercies and grandeurs?" (*ibid.*). The root of such thinking is an inadequate esteem for our nature. "Since we do not prize souls as is deserved by creatures made in the image of God we do not understand the deep secrets that lie in them" (*ibid.*).

Indeed there is yet more to be revealed, for now the Lord brings us into the deepest recesses of the castle.

> When our Lord is pleased to have pity on this soul that He has taken spiritually as His Spouse because of what it suffers and has suffered through its desires. He brings it, before the spiritual marriage is consummated, into His dwelling place which is this seventh. For just as in heaven so in the soul His Majesty must have a room where He dwells alone. Let us call it another heaven (VII,1:3).

This is the mansion of spiritual marriage. Union with God is complete and permanent. The experiences of this mansion go beyond any which have been encountered thus far. "Between the spiritual betrothal and the spiritual marriage the difference is as great as that which exists between two who are betrothed and two who can no longer be separated" (VII,2:2).

MARRIAGE

The union with God experienced in this dwelling place is significantly different than the grace of union in previous mansions. The precise difference is found in our understanding of the favor being granted. In the other mansions, "when God joins the soul to Himself, it doesn't understand anything; for all the faculties are lost" (VII,1:5).

> In this seventh dwelling place the union comes about in a different way: our good God now desires to remove the scales from the soul's eyes and let it see and understand, although in a strange way, something of the favor He grants it. When the soul is brought into that dwelling place, the Most Blessed Trinity, all three Persons, through an intellectual vision, is revealed to it through a certain representation of the truth. ... Through an admirable knowledge the soul understands as a most profound truth that all three Persons are one substance and one power and one knowledge and one God alone (VII,1:6).

Thus, the door to the seventh dwelling place is this intellectual vision of the Holy Trinity. Our awareness of the Trinity's presence is not a passing phenomenon. "Each day this soul becomes more amazed, for these Persons never seem to leave it any more, but it clearly beholds...that they are within it" (VII,1:7). In fact, "the soul finds itself in this company every time it takes notice" (VII,1:9). We could think that such a constant awareness of God's presence would create a kind of daze within us, leaving us incapable of attentiveness to anything else. "On the contrary, the soul is much more occupied than before with everything pertaining to the service of God; and once its duties are over it remains with that enjoyable company" (VII,1:8). Our sensitivity to and service of others intensify as we are drawn deeper into the castle. Any "spiritual" experiences which would produce a contradictory effect are not the work of God's presence and activity within us.

The spiritual marriage itself takes place when "His Majesty desires to show Himself to the soul through an imaginative vision of His most sacred humanity so that the soul will understand and not be ignorant of receiving this sovereign gift" (VII,2:1). Any subsequent, similar experiences come through an intellectual vision. God's purpose in this is clear, "He has desired to be so joined with the creature that, just as those who are married cannot be separated, He doesn't want to be separated from the soul" (VII,2:3).

With such a profound union, we could be tempted to think "that when the soul reaches this state in which God grants it this favor, it is sure of its salvation and safe from falling again" (VII,2:9). Saint Teresa makes it clear that this is not the case. In fact, we are more cautious than ever, guarding ourselves "from any small offense against God and with the strongest desires to serve Him" (*ibid.*). We are keenly aware of our complete dependence on God and therefore sense our inability and sometimes failure to respond to the abundant gifts which have been lavished upon us. Thus, "when this soul does penance, the delight will be greater in the measure that the penance is greater" (*ibid.*). Through this dependence on God, peacefulness is planted deep within us and remains undisturbed even though we can experience and be surrounded by trials and sufferings.

The principal challenge confronting us in the seventh mansion is simply to avoid all carelessness regarding our relationship with God. Because we have strong determination and strong desires not to offend God, we cannot thereby assume that we "fail to commit many imperfections, and even sins" (VII,4:3). We have no certitude that we are secure from failure. Saint Teresa's insight, then, is most wise: "To beseech God that we not offend Him is the greatest security we can have. May He be praised forever, amen" (*ibid.*).

PRAYER

Much of what has been said thus far directly concerns the nature and experience of prayer in the seventh mansion. This present section, then, will focus on the six effects of spiritual marriage identified by Saint Teresa.

"The first effect is a forgetfulness of self, for truly the soul, seemingly, no longer is" (VII,3:2). I want to do everything and direct all my energies in life to "procuring the honor of God" (*ibid.*). I no longer "want to be anything in anything, except when...the glory and honor of God may increase one degree" (*ibid.*). I see God's works so clearly that my own efforts seem as nothing. Still, I do everything necessary for daily life; I do not forget to eat or sleep or care for my health.

"The second effect is that the soul has a great desire to suffer" (VII,3:4). Previously, I experienced this desire as unsettling, now I accept that the Lord's will must be done at all costs. In fact, I "think everything His Majesty does is good. If He desires the soul to suffer, well and good; if not, it doesn't kill itself as it used to" (*ibid.*). Whatever God desires for me and whatever God does in my life are acceptable.

Third, "these souls also have a deep interior joy when they are persecuted" (VII,3:5). I see no value in becoming disturbed when others do not like me or when it seems they are making life particularly difficult for me. I harbor no "hostile feelings toward those who do, or desire to do, (me) evil" (*ibid.*). In fact, I strive to love them and would sacrifice the favors I have received if God "would bestow these same gifts on those others so that they wouldn't offend our Lord" (*ibid.*).

Fourth, seventh mansion dwellers "have just as great a desire to serve the Lord and that through them He be praised and that they may benefit some soul if they can" (VII,3:6). I want to be of service to God in every and any way possible. My "glory lies in being able some way to help the Crucified" (*ibid.*); I am willing to live many years with trials if this would give praise to God.

Fifth, "there is a great detachment from everything and a desire to be always either alone or occupied in something that will benefit some soul" (VII,3:8). I experience no interior trials or aridity; rather, I live "with a remembrance and tender love of our Lord" (*ibid.*). The Lord teaches me what I must do to be always pleasing to God and "almost always disposes the soul to be able to do what was said with a resolute will" (VII,3:9).

Sixth, "there is no fear that this sublime favor can be counterfeited by the devil, but the soul is wholly sure that the favor comes from God" (VII,3:10). I know that my own efforts, "faculties and senses have nothing to do with what goes on in this dwelling place" (*ibid.*). What I realize and experience is God's work within me; thus, there is no reason for me to make extensive efforts because God does all that is necessary.

These effects are not continuous, "for sometimes our Lord leaves these individuals in their natural state" (VII,4:1). But, Saint Teresa assures us that this does not last very long, "a day at most or a little more" (VII,4:2). Fortunately, whatever disturbances we experience because of this do not touch us on the deepest levels, "for the Lord gives the soul great stability and good resolutions not to deviate from His service in anything" (*ibid.*).

RELATIONSHIPS

Selfless service of God and others is the hallmark of life in the seventh mansion. Such service confirms that the favors we have received are indeed from God. There is an inseparable link between our actions in service and our prayer. Saint Teresa is quite explicit, "This is the reason for prayer...the purpose of this spiritual marriage: the birth always of good works, good works. This is the true sign of a thing, or favor, being from God" (VII,4:6-7).

My relationships are the primary and necessary arena in which I must live the graces I have received. Even though I do not always have an awareness that I can serve and help others, I strive to be as generous as possible. I have a genuine sense of union with all people. I am sensitive to others' needs and want to be of some assistance regardless of the cost to myself. Prayer itself enables me to serve and supports that service. As Teresa teaches, "let us desire and be occupied in prayer not for the sake of our enjoyment but so as to have this strength to serve" (VII,4:12).

I am focussed in serving and caring for others. However much I could and do desire to enrich the world, I recognize that I can only begin to fulfill that desire if I serve and care for those closest to me. They must remain the principal focus of my desire in this regard. As Saint Teresa says, "you need not be desiring to benefit the whole world but must concentrate on those who are in your company, and thus your deed will be greater since you are more obliged toward them" (VII,4:14).

For Teresa, the spiritual life can never be summed up by our experiences in prayer, actions must always be included. "It is necessary that your foundation consist of more than prayer and contemplation. If you do not strive for the virtues and practice them, you will always be dwarfs" (VII,4:9).

Our actions need not be monumental; their true value is not rooted in their extent but in our motivation.

> What I conclude with is that we shouldn't build castles in the air. The Lord doesn't look so much at the greatness of our works as at the love with which they are done. And if we do what we can, His Majesty will enable us each day to do more and more, provided that we do not quickly tire. ... Thus even though our works are small they will have the value our love for Him would have merited had they been great (VII,4:15).

ASSIMILATION

The experiences and favors within the seventh mansion express clearly the incarnational character of Teresian spirituality. The spiritual marriage is our assimilation into God. We understand "that it is God who gives life to our soul" (VII,2:6). All our experiences within the spiritual life have gradually drawn us toward this complete union precisely so we could be graced with living God's own life. "For it is very certain that in emptying ourselves of all that is creature and detaching ourselves from it for the love of God, the same Lord will fill us with Himself" (VII,2:7). By this union of our life with God's own, we imitate the Lord Jesus. Saint Teresa insists that this is the very reason God's favors are given.

> His Majesty couldn't grant us a greater favor than to give us a life that would be an imitation of the life His beloved Son lived. Thus I hold for certain that these favors are meant to fortify our weakness...that we may be able to imitate Him in His great sufferings (VII,4:4).

Assimilation into God, living God's own life, involves a complete union of lives and possessions. Saint Teresa recounts her own experience of spiritual marriage during which the Lord spoke "and told her that now it was time that she consider as her own what belonged to Him and that He would take care of what was hers" (VII,2:1). Later on she tells us, "it seems the words His Majesty spoke to her produced the deed in her. ... Thus, the soul doesn't worry about all that can happen" (VII,3:2). We are graced thereby with a confidence which rests firmly upon the surety of God's constant and loving presence and activity within us.

This entire journey, the interior castle itself, "has humility as its foundation. If humility is not genuinely present, for your own sake the Lord will not construct a high building lest that building fall to the ground" (VII,4:8). Even here, in these central rooms of the castle, Saint Teresa echoes what she taught us in the very first mansion. "While we are on this earth nothing is more important to us than humility" (I,2:9).

These reflections will close with the prayer which concludes Saint Teresa's own presentation of the seventh dwelling place. Let us pray with her.

> May it please His Majesty...that we all reach that place where we may ever praise Him. Through the merits of His Son who lives and reigns forever and ever, may He give me the grace to carry out something of what I tell you, amen (VII,4:16).

"IN EACH OF THESE THERE ARE MANY OTHERS"

CONCLUSION

"In each of these there are many others." At the very beginning of the *Interior Castle* Saint Teresa taught us that "our soul is like a castle in which there are many rooms, just as in heaven there are many dwelling places" (I,1:1). The Teresian doctrine underlying this rich imagery is that there are many pathways to assimilation into God. Not everyone will go through exactly the same rooms, not everyone will have exactly the same experiences, not everyone will follow precisely the same time line. Ultimately, the spiritual journey is God's work within us, the work which leads us ever more deeply into the paschal mystery.

Teresa presents seven mansions, then, not as a law for what must happen in the spiritual life, but as a model to highlight the main lines of our journey toward complete union with God. There can be and are other mansions; thus, she tells us,

> Although no more than seven dwelling places were discussed, in each of these there are many others, below and above and to the sides, with lovely gardens and fountains and labyrinths, such delightful things that you would want to be dissolved in praises of the great God who created the soul in His own image and likeness (*Epilogue*, 3).[1]

---

[1]. The *Epilogue* to the *Interior Castle* was originally a letter which accompanied Saint Teresa's manuscript when it was mailed to the sisters in Seville.

PATTERN OF THE MANSIONS

Pecisely because "there are many others," the seven mansions serve as a model, revealing a pattern which teaches us the fundamental principles of Teresian spirituality.

In the first dwelling place, the mansion of self-knowledge, we experience the beginnings of our spiritual journey. We learn the importance of making serious efforts to keep our spiritual life alive and active. Since prayer is the door to this mansion, our primary response must be fidelity. However simple our prayer, however sparse our spiritual practices, we must remain faithful if we truly desire to progress along the pathways of the journey.

The second dwelling place, the mansion of understanding desire, is a period of growth in the spiritual journey. The efforts we made in the first mansion, and even now continue to make, must be accompanied by our desire to progress. Renunciation of whatever could interfere with our relationship with the Lord is the door to this mansion, determination to maintain the quality of that relationship must mark our response.

In the third dwelling place, the mansion of self-renunciation, we take up the death to self which confirms the fidelity and determination flowing from our experiences in the preceding mansions. Perseverance and God's mercy form the door to this mansion, we must respond now in obedience to whatever God asks of us, to whatever God's will holds in store for us.

These first three mansions are within the active or natural part of the spiritual journey. Our movement through them is driven by our efforts in response to God's presence and activity within us. These three mansions open us to God's will and work within us. Under our own power we can go no further. We are led toward and drawn into the remaining mansions by God. We are not thereby stripped of our ability to make efforts, but we do have an increasing and intensifying awareness that even with those efforts, "all that we have done, Lord, you have done for us" (Isaiah 26:12). Living that awareness is necessary as we are brought into the central rooms of the castle; that is, the remaining four mansions, the passive or supernatural part of the spiritual journey. As Saint Teresa teaches us, "you will not be able to enter all the dwelling places through your own efforts, even though these efforts may seem to you great, unless the Lord of the castle Himself brings you there" (*Epilogue*, 2).

The fourth dwelling place, the mansion of quiet, is a time of new beginnings. The death to self planted in the third mansion has now become the seed of new life. God's gift of the prayer of quiet is the door to this mansion. Our response, also a gift, is attentiveness, to be alert to and disposed for whatever God does, wherever God leads. Quiet enables us to be still before God and open to God.

In the fifth dwelling place, the mansion of union, we experience a more profound growth and movement toward complete unity with God. The gift of the prayer of union is the door to this mansion and we respond by our diligence in practicing all the truths the Lord is teaching us, following all the ways the Lord is leading us. Our desire to be one with God and our love for God must be incarnated by our dependence upon God in everything.

The sixth dwelling place, the mansion of betrothal, leads us to a pervasive death to self. God must become the absolute center of our life. Thus, everything within us which is not of God must be put to death. God draws us toward this death to self through the trials and sufferings which constitute the door to this mansion. Also, many are the favors received within this dwelling place. The gift of courage enables us to trust God's work within us, the very work which leads us from death to new life.

In the seventh dwelling place, the mansion of marriage, we are graced with that new life of complete union with God. This grace is ratified by an intellectual vision of the Trinity which is the door to this mansion and by an imaginative vision of Jesus' humanity through which the spiritual marriage takes place. All is God's work here, we are assimilated into God, we live in union with God's own life.

There is a two-fold pattern evident in the seven dwelling places. First, in our journey through the first three mansions to the remaining four there is a pattern of the general movement from the natural and active aspects of the spiritual life to those which are supernatural and passive. Second, there is a double pattern of beginnings, growth, and death to self. In the first three mansions, this pattern reflects our work; in the next three mansions, it flows from God's work. The seventh dwelling place stands apart as the culmination of all this by the grace of our permanent union with God.

NATURAL - ACTIVE	SUPERNATURAL - PASSIVE
1. Self-Knowledge Beginnings	4. Quiet New Beginnings
2. Understanding Desire Growth	5. Union Profound Growth
3. Self-Renunciation Death to Self	6. Betrothal Death to Self - Life for God
	7. Marriage Complete Union with God

MANSIONS AS MODEL

Saint Teresa's *Interior Castle* with its seven mansions presents a model of the spiritual life. Teresa provides us with a clear perspective on the dynamics of being led and drawn by the Lord toward union with God. Even though this model is at the very foundations of the Church's mystical tradition, it cannot be applied indiscriminately. It is important to reiterate here a point made in the first chapter. The *Interior Castle* is an experiential model, not the result of a scientific experiment. It cannot be used as a gauge to judge ourselves or others in terms of spiritual progress, nor as a criterion to determine precisely which mansion we are currently experiencing in life.

This point is especially important since prayer and relationships were used as the lenses through which the practical nature of each dwelling place was viewed. We cannot assume there will be a perfectly timed parallelism between our spiritual growth and our relational development. Only general principles were presented, there will surely be discrepancies depending upon our personality and capabilities. Our prayer may advance without the corresponding development in our relational life; likewise, our relationships can reflect more maturity and stability than our commitment to and practice of prayer. However, even though perfect parallelism is not a realistic principle, the discrepancy between our prayer and our relationships cannot be so great as to preclude any level of correspondence between them.

IDENTITY, DIRECTION, MEANING

The seven mansions begin in self-knowledge and end with our assimilation into God. Saint Teresa of Avila expertly guides us along the pathways of this journey to identity and direction and meaning in life. Who am I? Where am I going? Why? She teaches us that the answers to these probing questions are simple, the challenge is to accept the answers as true. And then, to live that truth. God's grace will do the rest.

Who am I? - created in the image and likeness of the living God, with the capacity to be completely one with God. This is my true identity in life. Everything else I cling to obscures this simple truth and hinders my efforts to realize and live it fully.

Where am I going? - toward that complete unity with God, by my efforts and by God's grace. This is my true direction in life, it is for this that I was created. Everything else I set up as a goal merely slows my progress.

Why? - because God loves me and desires to be one with me, and that I be one with God. This is my true meaning in life. Everything else I claim as essential shields me from the beckoning warmth of that love.

As we journey toward union with God, many things - valuable realities - will compete for a place in our heart, thus influencing our identity, direction, and meaning in life. The extent of that influence will be determined by the place and priority we allow them to take. If those realities, however valuable, are permitted to displace the centrality of God in our life, then we will create a multitude of barriers and detours in our journey to God. We will have answers to the questions, but they will be insufficient to match our dignity as creatures of a loving God. Our heart will wander aimlessly, unsatisfied, until once again we are grounded firmly in the Lord who dwells deep within us.

"WALK THROUGH IT AT ANY TIME"

Through her teaching in the *Interior Castle*, Saint Teresa reminds us of God's intimacy with us and accessibility to us. God is within, we need only begin the journey inward to be drawn toward union. The castle is ours to explore, God's loving and merciful grace will lead us and accompany us along its pathways. Thus, Teresa assures us that "you can enter and take a walk through it at any time" (*Epilogue*, 1). With such firm and encouraging assurance from this Doctor of the Church, we should not hesitate to begin the journey. "Once you get used to enjoying this castle, you will find rest in all things, even those involving much labor, for you will have the hope of returning to the castle which no one can take from you" (*Epilogue*, 2).

Saint Teresa tells us "now that I am finished (writing this book) I admit the work has brought me much happiness" (*Epilogue*, 1). And we know, too, her work has brought much wisdom and insight to countless individuals over the past four centuries and to the Church itself. No doubt, it will continue to do so.

This book will conclude with the request which Saint Teresa makes near the very end of her writing. "I ask that each time you read this work you, in my name, praise His Majesty fervently and ask for the increase of His Church...May our God be forever praised and blessed, amen, amen" (*Epilogue*, 4).

INDEX